Contents

Contents

'HURRY HURRY'

Photo: Albert thrilling the Elland Road crowd

"A trailblazer and inspiration to black footballers across the world." Brazilian superstar Pele's verdict on Albert Johanneson.

Portuguese Legend Eusébio (The Black Panther) said of Albert: "Generations of black footballers should look to Albert Johanneson and thank him for what he achieved."

Leeds United's most successful manger, Don Revie: "He could do things with a football that most players I knew could only dream of."

Justin Fashanu: "Every black footballer of a generation knows of Albert, his football skills are legend."

Billy Bremner: "He had so much pace and strength, he was a great athlete."

INTRODUCTION

I had the honour of meeting the great Albert 'Hurry Hurry' Johanneson at Leeds United's home ground of Elland Road in the summer of 1990. I was on a coaching course to gain my FA Preliminary Coaching Badge and was a part of the Leeds United Football in the Community scheme which was run by the charismatic Ces Podd.

Ces had previously had his own successful professional career playing at Bradford City from 1970 to 1984. He would go on to become Bradford's record appearance holder with 565 appearances.

Ces had moved to Leeds from St Kitts in the West Indies as a child and would go watch Leeds United at nearby Elland Road. Ces's love of football was inspired by his visits to Elland Road and of seeing Albert in particular. He said of his visits to Elland Road:

"It was magic. He (Albert) was magic. The only reason I went to Elland Road in the first place, to be the only black kid in the crowd, was because of Albert. That's a fact."

Although he saw Albert as a great player, he said of Albert's temperament: "It was like he felt he had to be really humble or show people he knew he was privileged. Lucky, even. The arrogance you need to be the best was missing because, to put it bluntly, there were people who didn't want him to be there. I think he felt that pressure."

When Ces introduced me to Albert he was sat alone in the waiting area outside Leeds United's large glass trophy cabinet. He was looking into the cabinet at the gleaming trophies from past glories.

At the time Albert was struggling and had come to Leeds United asking for financial support. As a genuine and caring man Ces was able to help Albert to furnish his flat.

Ces himself, throughout his long football career had the misfortune to be the target of racist 'supporters' and knew how much Albert had suffered in the past. Knowing Albert's story and that he had fallen on hard times he wanted to help an ex-professional like himself who he had looked up to from the terraces.

After being introduced to Albert, I was in awe of a Leeds United legend knowing he had been the first black player to appear in an FA Cup Final in its then 93-year history in 1965, and who had been instrumental in the rapid rise of Leeds United throughout the 1960s. He was at the start of Leeds United's rise to the top of English football after becoming the first signing of the new Leeds United manager Don Revie, who would go on to give Leeds domestic and European glory.

As I sat in conversation with the legendary flying left-winger, I was struck by how shy and reticent he was to talk about his magnificent career and how a true hero to so many was so self-effacing and appearing to lack in confidence. After all this was a man who had been an exciting and pioneering player, who had starred alongside some of the greatest footballers to grace English football. I was aware that Albert had been through a struggle with alcohol and my perception was that there was a distant sadness behind his eyes, but for me, meeting Albert was a privilege, not only in meeting a man who had gone through so much in his early days living in apartheid South Africa, but who had also faced a lot of prejudice and racism while making his way as a young man in England.

My own feeble attempt at a professional football career had amounted to no more than a handful of games for Huddersfield Town juniors and one solitary appearance for their reserves in a 4-0 thumping at West Bromwich Albion in 1980. I was therefore intrigued with Albert's journey, his rise and then gradual fall from the top of English football.

Although at times it makes for uncomfortable reading, his story, interspersed with the stories of many other pioneering black footballers makes for a fascinating read. There are terms and insults throughout the book that should never have been uttered, but to truly understand what the original black pioneers of the game faced, they are repeated as they were quoted. Through his own words, and that of his contemporaries in interviews, newspaper reports and television commentaries Albert's story can be relived and celebrated. It also includes a chronological run through of all his 199 appearances (171 league, 28 cup) for Leeds United.

Albert was a player who blazed a trail for generations of black English footballers. And although his achievements were not fully recognised at the time, he is still revered today in acknowledgement of his enormous contribution through such difficult times.

Photo: Albert in his early days at Leeds

EARLY DAYS IN APARTHEID SOUTH AFRICA

Albert Louis Johanneson was born on 13 March 1940 in Germiston, South Africa. Germiston is a small city in the East Rand region of Guatang with a population of approx. 250,000 people. An interesting fact about Germiston is that it is currently South Africa's sixth largest city and has 70% of the western world's gold passing through its gold refinery. It also has a British connection having been established in the early days of the gold rush by two prospectors, namely John Jack from the town of Germiston near Glasgow and August Simmer from Vacha in Germany.

John and August struck paydirt on the farm of Elandsfontein, with John naming the place Germiston after his childhood home near Glasgow. Both men made their fortunes in the mines and from their discovery and influx of new workers, Germiston was founded.

Growing up in apartheid South Africa, Albert was described from an early age as an introverted and shy boy. His demeanour was made worse as he faced the constant threat of racism and segregation which weighed heavily upon him.

As a young child he faced daily racist taunts and abuse, with one particular event leaving a lifelong impression on him. Albert told the story of when he was around six years of age playing out with friends on the street, when a car stopped close to him and a white boy approximately the same age as Albert leaned out and spat in Albert's face. Albert said he froze in shock and fear, unperturbed the boy laughed and repeated the vile act. To compound the sickening insult, the driver of the car reached out and struck Albert across his neck with what Albert described as 'something like a long horse whip'. His friends ran off in a panic, Albert lay on the ground trying to protect himself but the man showed no mercy and kicked Albert before making a cowardly get away. Dazed and shocked Albert lay motionless unable to comprehend what had happened before finally managing to get back on his feet and running home as fast as his legs would carry him.

This particular attack as well as many other forms of racist abuse that Albert faced on a daily basis made an already shy and bashful boy reticent with fear. His upbringing in apartheid South Africa would play a big part in his development, leaving him with a nervous disposition which he carried throughout his life.

Albert said of the apartheid movement in South Africa: "No set of human beings has the right to treat another like we 'blacks' and 'coloureds' as they called us. We couldn't walk on the same streets as them, speak to them, shop in the same stores, or live and go to the same areas where they lived or visited. As young children we were soft targets and were punished if we dared to breathe the same air as white people, it was ridiculous."

Another shocking incident left its mark on Albert when he was witness to an attack on his car mechanic father, Louis. Albert explained: "I saw two white men walk into the garage. No words were exchanged. My father asked them what they wanted. The men approached him and without any provocation, they attacked him, punching him to the floor. It was terrifying to watch these very violent and very angry strangers beating my father. I desperately wanted to do something to stop it, to help him, but I knew I couldn't. If they knew I was there they would take me away and kill me."

He continued: “If anyone dared to stand up to white oppressors they suffered serious consequences.”

Albert recalls that a friend of his named Archie disappeared one night along with his whole family. The family was never seen again. The disappearance happened after Archie’s cobbler father had refused to repair two white man’s shoes the day before. Albert was convinced that the full family of seven had been murdered. According to Albert this was a regular occurrence in the deprived black areas of Germiston and indeed throughout Johannesburg.

Although not drawn to football at an early age, Albert found running as a way of freedom and release. He began running when he was around six, he said: “It was all barefoot, there was no such thing available to us as a training shoe or running track, I lost the number of times I sliced open the soles of my feet on broken glass.” But he said of running, “I ran like the wind. It made me feel free, unchained, almost like I was flying like a bird. If you can run like the wind, you had more chance of escaping the oppressors.” Albert would also use his youthful athletic prowess to help his father’s garage to survive. He would risk a beating by entering white areas after dark to steal parts from parked cars that his father would be able to use on the cars he was fixing. Albert said he did this without his father’s knowledge but said his father must have known when car parts would just appear! Around this time Albert also confessed to something he said he was later ashamed of. He said to escape the reality of everyday beatings and abuse, he and his brother, Trevor, along with other friends would resort to sniffing benzene (a type of petrol) through jars. He said the high they got was a type of escape with the vapours making everyone feel very happy and carefree…until it began to wear off, causing headaches and tearful eyes. He said he stopped after the death of one of his friends he called 'Nervous Norman', who died from the effects.

With encouragement from his friends, Albert entered his teenage years running along the uneven rocky roads of Germiston with a tennis ball at his bare feet, perfecting his ball control while constantly trying new tricks. Albert said of his gift: "The ball and I were as one and I would challenge people to try take it from me. They couldn't as I would twist and turn and spin round then sprint off, the ball still at my feet. I became a bit of a local act and people came from all over Germiston to bet money on whether I could achieve more difficult tasks with the ball. Not that I saw any money, it was always others who did the gambling. I was tasked with more and more new challenges and with these came time limitations to achieve them a small crowd would shout at me 'Hurry Hurry' a name that stuck with me in Germiston as I became known as Albert 'Hurry Hurry' Johanneson."

His ability with a ball began to get noticed, and although he had received rough treatment from uncompromising defenders which had deterred him in his early attempt at competitive football, when his local team (Shamrocks) found themselves a player short he was persuaded to play for them.

With Albert not having any football boots, he played barefoot but still gave a man of the match performance. With the game evenly balanced at 1-1 he scored a wonderful solo goal which won the game with only two minutes to go. He said of the match: "My team went wild with excitement, I was mobbed by them and chaired off the pitch as an acknowledgement for my performance, I was thrilled."

This enthused Albert, his delicate demeanour was strengthened and a passion for football was ignited. Albert would shine for his school team in Germiston and was selected to play for Germiston Caledonian Society Amateur Football Club (later to be called Germiston Callies F.C).

Germiston Callies was formed in 1906 by Scottish immigrants who had migrated to work in the mines and on the railways. The club changed its name in 1959 when it turned professional and boasted of having a future Liverpool captain, Berry Nieuwenhuys ('Nivvy') in its side in the early 1930s. Nivvy would go to play 239 times for Liverpool scoring 74 goals between 1933 and 1947.

With Albert continuing to impress playing for Germiston Coloured School, he was selected to represent the coloured national team in the Kajee Cup Final (named after A I Kajee a politician in the National Indian Congress). The Kajee Cup was a biennial national inter-race tournament called the A.I. Kajee Cup which was organised by the South African Soccer Federation (SASF) and ran from 1952-1966. Albert said of his appearance for the national coloured team: "It was a great time for me, I was young enough to have the stamina and fit enough to run around for hours at a time. A white British coach called 'Topper' Brown was the manager, he had not an ounce of malice nor was he culturally biased in any way. He loved football and wanted us to enjoy it too, he would tell us to play it naturally, let the ball do the work. I won the Kajee cup twice, once in 1956 and again in 1960. I was captain and it was a real honour and achievement."

Around this time Albert played in the same football side as the legendary South African cricketer Basil D'Oliveira whose selection for the England Test team to tour South Africa in 1968-69 caused uproar, with the South

African government headed by John Vorster banning him. This led to the tour being cancelled and South Africa being exiled from international cricket until the fall of apartheid in 1994. Basil said of Albert: "He was a wonderfully gifted footballer, possibly the best player to ever come out of South Africa. He was the unsung hero of that era and I am proud to say I played alongside him in football games."

Albert had begun to gain attention from English clubs with his outstanding displays of skill and breath-taking speed. Unbeknown to him, a local school teacher and football coach from the small town of Benoni called Barney Gaffney had begun to watch him playing for the school team. Gaffney said of the time he watched Albert: "What shocked me was when he (Albert) dribbled (past) four players from the Bloemfontein team, and it was then that I thought that this man doesn't belong here, he must go and play overseas."

Gaffney eventually approached Albert and offered to help him with his game. Gaffney wanted to push Albert to reach his full potential and with his encouragement and coaching he knew he would have an outstanding chance to become a professional footballer in England. Albert said: "I had heard of Barney Gaffney, and knew him as one of the most respected black scouts in the region. I wasn't sure I was good enough, but Barney and I worked on all aspects of my game. My legs would ache after each session, yet I could see that they were growing stronger. Barney was a fine man and I really respected him for giving me his time and constantly pushing me. He tried to get me to change all aspects of my life, smoking drinking and the food I would eat. I enjoyed a smoke and liked my food and we couldn't really afford to choose my diet so that was the end of the matter."

The smoking and diet didn't stop Albert from progressing and eventually Gaffney became aware of interest in Albert from teams in England, most notably Newcastle United and Leeds United. Newcastle initially approached Albert with their interest and said they would be back in touch, but nothing came of it.

Meanwhile Gaffney was as good as his word and arranged a three-month trial for Albert with Leeds United in January 1961. Gaffney's main challenge was to convince Albert to take the giant step of uprooting and leaving his family and the only life he had known behind in South Africa. Albert was in a close knit family, he had brothers and sisters and was especially close to his mother and father (Caroline and Louis) who were very protective.

Although growing up in a racist apartheid society, the townships of Johannesburg and the Transvaal areas were all that Albert had known. Leaving the area, let alone the country, was a major decision for Albert to make. Everyone Albert spoke to was filled with joy and excitement for him, but he remained nervous about leaving everything behind. With further encouragement from his family and the encouragement and support from Barney Gaffney, Albert took the big decision to accept the trial and move to England. Albert had no misdemeanours on his record, having never been caught by the authorities committing any anti-establishment acts and so was given authorisation to travel to England. One of the proviso's that Albert was given was that he must not return to South Africa 'destitute or with any liabilities', a condition he found ironic considering what he was leaving behind. So the decision was made and Albert would make the long trip to England in the hope of making a better life.

SOUTH AFRICA'S APARTHEID SPORTS POLICY

The South African Minister of the Interior, Theophilus Ebenhaezer Dönges (1898-1968) was described as one of the masterminds behind South Africa's Apartheid Sports Policy in 1956. The policy attempted to discourage mixed-race sports teams in South Africa with its segregation laws, making it nigh on impossible for black players like Steve Mokone and Albert Johanneson to forge a career in sport within South Africa. Although there was a move to create a racially integrated football league, the South African Football Association denied access to municipal grounds for anyone outside of their jurisdiction, severely restricting any attempt at integrated football.

The racist apartheid policy also stated that any foreign countries wanting to play international games in South Africa were only allowed to do so if they only sent all-white teams. FIFA's 1960 Rome Congress passed a resolution in which national associations could not practice racial, religious or political discrimination. The whites-only South African Soccer Federation (FASA) was given twelve months to abide by the resolution.

At the start of the 1960s attitudes were beginning to change, the Sharpeville massacre showed the world the horrors of racist policies. The massacre on 21 March 1960 happened in the Black township of Sharpeville, near Johannesburg, South Africa. Afrikaner police opened fire on a group of unarmed Black South African demonstrators, killing 69 people and wounding 180 in a hail of submachine-gun fire. The demonstrators were protesting against the South African government's restriction of non-white travel and the pass laws. In the aftermath of the Sharpeville massacre, protests broke out in Cape Town with a state of emergency being declared. More than 10,000 people were arrested before government troops restored order and the Pan-Africanist Congress (PAC) who had organised the demonstration, and the African National Congress (ANC) were outlawed.

The FASA were still unwilling to change its racist position. But the Sharpeville massacre had shocked the world and had put more pressure on the International Federation of Association Football (FIFA) to take action.

In late September 1961, the 67 FIFA member states met in London, eventually responding to South Africa's apartheid regime by suspending them from international football. It was the first step in what would become a much wider boycott with South Africa being banned from the Olympic Games in 1964 and international cricket in 1970.

The sports boycott would gradually expand into a wider cultural boycott, and by the late 1980s tough economic sanctions were imposed on South Africa. With apartheid being dismantled, South Africa was allowed to rejoin Fifa in 1992.

THE PATH FROM SOUTH AFRICA TO ENGLAND

Albert's path to England as a black footballer had been lightly trod. There had been white South Africans in the Football league previously including Bolton's Wilfred Waller in 1900, and in 1903 Manchester United's Alex Bell. The English and Scottish leagues were well represented by white South Africans in the 1930s, most notably the prolific goal scorer, Gordon Hodgson (1904-1951) who scored 295 goals in 467 games in England, at Liverpool 1925-1936 (358 app 233 goals) Aston Villa 1936-1937 (28 app 11 goals) and Leeds United 1937-1939 (81 app 51 goals). He was also capped twice by South Africa and three times for England.

Photo: Gordon Hodgson

Even though there had been a steady stream of white South African players in both the English and Scottish leagues, it wouldn't be until 1956 before a black player would arrive from South Africa to play in Britain, when Steve Mokone landed in England to play for Coventry City.

The 1948 Nationality Act made it easier for British clubs to induce colonial players to sign for them. The act guaranteed colonial and Commonwealth citizen's the right of entry to the UK subject to the status that they could also play for the national team. This created a willingness for British clubs to trial and sign South African footballers, but the thought at the time was that only white players would be able to settle in Britain and fit into the character of a tough dressing room environment.

This made white players keenly sought after, with first division Charlton Athletic leading the way having five white South Africans on their payroll at the same time. Steve Mokone was the first Black South African to be allowed a passport to play abroad giving him official approval to travel.

Between 1956 and 1961 only three black players in England were signed from apartheid South Africa, Stephen Mokone (1932-2015), Gerry Francis (b.1933) and Albert Johanneson. Although it had become possible, the passage to Britain for Black footballers was curtailed even further with the gradual enforcement of the 1962, 1968 and 1971 immigration acts, which had the aim of the restricting immigration of all Commonwealth passport holders. Prospective immigrants were increasingly unable to enter purely as Commonwealth citizens and needed to apply for a work voucher. The vouchers were usually only given to high-skilled workers such as doctors.

In 1962, the governing Conservative Party wanted a control on mass migration and issued a limited number of government-issued employment vouchers, the Leader of the Opposition, Labour's Hugh Gaitskell called the government's legislation "cruel and brutal anti-colour legislation."

STEVE MOKONE – THE FIRST BLACK AFRICAN TO PLAY PROFESSIONALLY IN EUROPE

Photo: Steve Mokone

Steve Mokone (nicknamed Kalamazoo after a Glenn Miller tune) became the first black African to play professionally in Europe.

Mokone lived a fascinating and eventful life, which is worthy of re-telling. After initially being held back by red tape, 23 year-old Mokone was eventually allowed a passport by the South African government to travel to England in 1956 for trials, on the proviso that 'he stayed out of politics, or else'. On arriving to London by flight, as a young black man entering the country for the first time the whole experience came as a major culture shock for Mokone. Britain was a completely different world to what he had experienced in Apartheid South Africa, and he later said of his early days in London:

"I'd never been in an all-white environment before, I had no one as a mentor. I had no one to talk to, no one to confide in. It was a very lonely experience. There were white people serving me in the restaurant and white people making my bed. It was a total culture shock."

Upon moving from London to Coventry, Mokone was placed in lodgings with a devoutly religious white family, with his arrival creating a buzz around the area. He soon became a local celebrity mainly due to his colour, he remembered children running up to him to touch him and that people would just stare. He later recalled: “It felt uncomfortable using the same cups and the same toilet as a white family, but these were problems of my own making, my cultural baggage."

Mokone made his historic debut on 13 October 1956 in front of a large crowd of 20,261 for a Division Three South game between Coventry City and Millwall at Highfield Road which Millwall won 2-1. Mokone would go on to make a further 3 appearances for Coventry, scoring one goal in a 4-1 win over Gillingham. Although he had been warned, Mokone found it difficult to stay out of politics, and through a friend of his family who was a senior figure in the African National Congress, William Nkono, his political interest continued to grow. Mokone said: "Dr Nkono, who was like a second father to me, said that every goal I scored would be one more goal towards independence." He recalled: "There were doubts and tears. I had reservations. But this was a chance of a lifetime to show that South Africa was not a bad place."

When manager Harry Warren left Coventry in 1957 by ‘mutual consent’ Mokone was out of favour and was given a free transfer to Heracles Almelo FC in the Netherlands. In 1959, he moved back to the Football League with Second Division Cardiff City. He played only three games however, scoring the opening goal in a 3-2 win over Liverpool.

After receiving an ankle injury Mokone was asked by Cardiff to play through the injury but he refused and was subsequently transferred to

Barcelona. After a short spell at Barcelona, he had further spells on loan in France with Marseille before moving onto to Torino in Italy. He moved back to Spain in 1961 with Valencia before joining Hamilton Steelers in Canad. He finished his football career in 1964 in Melbourne, Australia where he played for the Caroline Springs George Cross FC. After Australia, Mokone moved back to the USA where he gained a degree, a master's and then a doctorate, becoming an assistant professor in psychiatry.

Mokone had married Joyce Maaga but became estranged from his wife which resulted in an acrimonious battle for the custody of their daughter, Thandi. Mokone who was a respected academic, won custody of his daughter as Maaga, who was a nurse, was deemed in a less favourable position as she was living in hospital accommodation.

From here the story turned ugly, as Mokone was allegedly attacked in a car park by three masked assailants. After the attack on November 20, 1977, lye a sodium Hydroxide was thrown into his ex-wife's face outside her Manhattan apartment. A week later, an almost identical attack with sulphuric acid left Maaga's lawyer, Ann Boylan Rogers, disfigured and blind in one eye. Mokone was arrested and charged with the attacks on the two women. Although Mokone always pledged that he didn't commit the crime, he pleaded guilty in a New Jersey court to the attack on his ex-wife and was sentenced to between eight and 12 years in jail.

In 1980, a New York court also convicted him of orchestrating the attack on Ann Rogers after he allegedly payed one of his former patients to throw sulphuric acid in her face.

The court sentenced him to between five and 15 years. Mokone's biographer, Dutch journalist Tom Egbers alleges in his book, *De Zwarte*

Meteoor (The Black Meteor) that Mokone had been framed by the US authorities in collaboration with the South African Department of Internal Affairs (DIA) due to Mokone becoming politically active and a prominent member of the African National Congress (ANC).

The US authorities considered the ANC to be a terrorist organisation and alleged that Mokone had been voicing his opposition to South Africa's apartheid regime in articles he wrote for a New York left wing journal.

Egbers accuses the authorities of framing Mokone by saying: "I managed to get hold of a hypnosis interview done by the CIA with his ex-wife and it is really incredible to hear how things are manipulated. After about 30 minutes of the interview, she is convinced that it was Steve (Mokone) who had attacked her but she is terribly led by the investigators. Those tapes were never used in the trial because it was obvious they were not admissible. There is also correspondence that shows the FBI and CIA dug into this matter. Now if you commit a crime, that doesn't usually happen. You will be arrested and you will go to trial but why would the CIA look into Steve Mokone? Everything was done to make people testify against him. For instance, Steve's son Ronnie Sello didn't have a US passport but was living there. They told him that, if he didn't testify, then he would be thrown out of the country and that's what he had to do. It was terrible. He had to testify against his own father."

Egbers continued: "Steve was married to an American woman called Louise, who is now his widow, and they wanted to stay in the US, he feared that if he ever said anything about what happened then he would have to leave. So he never spoke about it." Mokone had celebrity support while in prison, with prominent figures like Desmond Tutu calling for an early release, but Mokone wasn't released until August 1990 after he had served 12 years in prison.

Mokone died in Washington aged 82 in 2015. His death was covered extensively in the Netherlands and South Africa's players wore black armbands in a friendly against Nigeria to commemorate someone who was seen as one of their most important pioneers. Following a ceremony at Johannesburg's FNB Stadium, the ashes of the man described as "our flag bearer in all the corners of the world" by the sports minister, Fikile Mbalula, were scattered in his homeland.

As is usual though in this type of story, there were two sides to the tale. After Mokone's death, his daughter Thandi Mokone-Chase wrote an article in the New York Times on July 30 2015, in which she said: "My father, Stephen "Kalamazoo" Mokone, was the first black South African soccer player to play professionally in Europe and to break the color barrier in South Africa during apartheid, which was a remarkable achievement back then. But he was more than that; he was also a violent and abusive man." She went on to say: "As a famous sports figure, my father had many admirers who overlooked his violent side, or even argued that he had been framed. My father's biographer, Tom Egbers, wrote that my father's conviction was part of a conspiracy involving South Africa's government and U.S. authorities. Egbers was convinced that Stephen Mokone was framed and convicted because he had participated as a young man in anti-apartheid activities. That's just not the case. Since my father's death, for the first in my life, I no longer feel silenced by my fear of him. I've been asked about my desire to "come out" of my silence and "why now?" I am speaking out. His passing has set me free to tell the truth; I can finally own my anger without fear of reprisal. There is very little now that can penetrate the emotional scars I suffered by my father's torment, which included: being physically abused and sexualized; choking my dog in front of me; and hiring an attacker who knocked out my brother's front teeth with the butt of a gun because he became a witness for the prosecution, giving sworn testimony that eventually incriminated our father. He was lauded as "a national asset" and "a hidden hero" but the violent, criminal acts for which he was responsible were minimized — if even mentioned. His narrative seems a representation of the violent athlete misogynist, similar to other elite athletes such as Floyd Mayweather, Ray Rice and Oscar Pistorius. How can it be that we excuse abusive behaviour with statements such as: "With the pressure of divorce and child custody battle…he simply lost his head," or "Good men sometimes do bad things?"

She finishes by saying: "Stephen 'Kalamazoo' Mokone was referred to as the "Black Meteor" in the Netherlands and "the Maserati" in Italy. While my father may have been a great soccer player, he was no hero in my life."

His daughter's revelations divided opinions at his old club Heracles in the Netherlands who had named one of their stands at their Polman Stadium, as well as a street being named after him. Heracles chairman, Jan Smit said after Thandi's New York Times article, "I am very shocked by the news, they are nasty accusations. He is now deceased, the case should be properly sorted out after that incriminating letter. Whether a stand in our new stadium will be renamed after him now is part of government consultation." With opinions divided, Mokone will still go down in history as the first Black South African to play professional football in Europe

ALBERT ARRIVES IN ENGLAND

When Albert was asked if he would be interested in following in Steve Mokone's footsteps to England with a three-month trial at Leeds United he was both delighted and terrified, he also had to confess that he had never heard of Leeds. On finding out that Leeds were a professional team who played in the English Football League second division, and already had a black South African footballer on their books named, Gerry Francis, Albert agreed to the trial.

The deal was that Leeds would arrange to give Albert a wage to cover his costs while he was on trial with them and provide him with food and lodgings. The downside to the deal was that Albert would have to part fund the travel expense to Leeds himself. He knew the money for the flight would be an issue, but his coach Barney Gaffney said if he wanted to go he would help to finance the trip to England. Albert said: "Everyone was thrilled and excited, everyone except me that is. I remained nervous about leaving behind everything I knew, everything I had grown up with, my family, my friends, my country."

After much thought he finally decided to go ahead and take the challenge, and although scared of flying he was excited at the new adventure that lay ahead. Albert said he was shaking and sweating when it came to boarding the plane, he was nauseous and sick several times before the plane even took off.

He confessed that he went through every emotion possible during the flight, elation, sadness and fear and not for the first time he said he couldn't help but cry.

From an early age Albert had only known apartheid South Africa. The Population Registration Act of 1950 had classified all South Africans as either Bantu (all Black Africans), Coloured (those of mixed race), or white. The apartheid system was based on the Group Areas Act in 1950 which established residential and business sections in each area for each race. This new act excluded thousands of Coloureds, Blacks and Indians from areas which were classified for white occupation only.

The result of these and previous acts resulted in more than 80 percent of South Africa's land being designated for the use of the white only minority. To implement the act in 1952, the government passed a stringent law that required all African men (there was strong opposition for it applying to women) age 16 and over to carry a 'reference book' (replacing a passbook that had previously been in force) which held their personal and employment information. The passbook was similar to a passport in that it contained detailed information about the individual, with employers (by law, an employer could only be a white person) being able to enter an evaluation of the pass holder's behaviour. The pass documented when permission was requested to be in a certain region and for what purpose, urban areas were considered 'White,' so a non-White person needed a passbook to be inside a city. Under apartheid, any governmental employee could remove these entries, which effectively refused permission for the person to stay in the area. If a passbook didn't have a valid entry, officials could arrest its owner and put him in prison. Africans often had to violate the pass laws to find work to support their families leaving them under the constant threat of harassment, fines and arrests. The passes became known as 'dompas' (dumb pass) and became the most hated and abhorrent symbol of apartheid. The passes weren't repealed until 1986 in which time more than 17 million people had been arrested.

Apartheid affected black people in every area of their lives, it was supposedly designed to allow different races to develop on their own, but in reality it forced Black South Africans into poverty and hopelessness. Everywhere from hospitals to beaches were segregated, education was limited and daily life was restricted in almost every facet for a black person.

Albert had lived all his life under this frightful regime, even his schooling was affected due to The Bantu Education Act (1953) which created state-run schools in which Black children were required to attend. The aim of the act was to train children for manual labour and menial jobs that the government deemed suitable for those of their race. For a loving but diffident person to leave his family and homeland for a whole new environment and culture was a frightening prospect, but Albert who was hoping for a better life, made the brave decision to leave the only home he had known and take the leap to travel to the distant shores of England.

On a cold Yorkshire morning in northern England on 5 January 1961, a shy 20 year-old Albert who had previously never set foot out of South Africa swapped the glorious sunshine to bring his exciting style of football to a snow covered Elland Road. At first the concept was very alien to him, and he was surprised at being able to mix equally with white people. After landing in London, his first introduction to life in England wasn't pleasant when a stranger bumped into him and insulted him by saying: "get out of the way nigger". Albert said: "I don't deny that incident hurt, it shattered my illusion of a better world." He was somewhat placated when a woman who had seen the incident and saw his distress offered him some words of comfort. Feeling very nervous and vulnerable, Albert was met at the terminal by the Leeds United's first team coach, Syd Owen. Syd had been a first class footballer himself, captaining the Luton Town team in their 1959 FA Cup Final defeat to Nottingham Forest in his final season as a player. The FA Cup win capped off a successful year in which he was also named the Football Writers Player of the Year. Syd gave Albert a warm welcome, which took Albert aback as he had never had a white man engage in so much conversation with him or show any concern as to his welfare.

Of the train journey to Leeds, Albert said: "I was shocked, stunned and a little frightened, people were so polite to me, smiling at me and engaging me in conversation on the train. They asked why I was over in England, I explained that I had come for work which raised a few eyebrows. I could see some people thinking that I had a cheek, leaving South Africa and coming to England to take their jobs. When I explained that I had come over for trials with Leeds United, it seemed to change perceptions and opinions, and suddenly I was wished every success."

Arriving by train in Leeds Albert said he felt cold the like of which he had never felt before, he said: "We went to a waiting black car, the driver opened the door for me and called me sir, it was the first time a white person had addressed me so." Albert was taken to Leeds United's Elland

Road ground and introduced to the Leeds manager, Jack Taylor. Albert said he felt immediately intimidated by Taylor, and recalled him saying to him: "The best way to understand and learn about Leeds is to listen and learn, once these people know who you are they will take to you, until then, you have to prove yourself to them and to me and the football club. I want no trouble from you, do you understand? If I do have problems, you'll be on that aeroplane back to South Africa on the same day." These were not the reassuring words that Albert wanted to hear.

Albert was given a look around the stadium, when he was told by the supporter giving him the tour: "We have another blackie here, he's called Gerry Francis. Do you come from the same village out there?"

Albert didn't think the man was being funny or nasty, rather that he was just ignorant and stupid.

Upon meeting up with Jack Taylor again, Albert curiously enquired as to whether black and white people were allowed to stand together in the stadium. Albert said that Taylor laughed and said: "Yes they can and do, but we don't have that many black people here Albert, I rarely see one in the city. You are unique not only to Leeds, but across the entire football profession here in Britain. It's not going to be easy for you to integrate, I can name maybe half a dozen black footballers who play professionally here. Many white people have a fear about your kind of people coming here, they see you as being very different to them. Someone has already asked me if you are a witch doctor. I have put that person in his place, he won't speak irresponsibly again. Your colour is going to be a real problem Albert, just don't let the bigots get to you, rise above the criticism about your skin colour, there's nothing wrong with you, you are an equal here as far as I and all the players and staff are concerned, but you will have to deal with rudeness and ignorance yourself. I cannot be shielding you 24 hours a day. Don't ever retaliate with violence, just rise above it, let your football skill be your response and do the talking for you, show them that you are better than them when it comes to the way they act."

With Taylor's words ringing in his ears, Albert was taken to his new home, a brick terraced house on Noster Hill in Beeston a suburb of Leeds which is only a five minute walk from the Elland Road stadium.

Edna Wineley was to be Albert's new landlady, a person he described as a warm caring woman who had a lovely smile and who made him feel at home straight away. Upon being shown his room, with time on his hands Albert decided to go for a run to familiarise himself with the area. With no training gear he ran around Beeston barefoot, but on returning to his digs he received a scalding from Mrs Wineley who said: "Albert, where have you been? Never go out in your bare feet again, you will damage yourself on those streets. If you hurt your feet you'll never get to play for Leeds United." He took Mrs Wineley's advice and didn't run barefoot again. But he would still go on regular runs around Beeston as a way of maintaining his fitness and it would help him to clear his mind.

He was still struggling with the cold and didn't own any clothes suitable for the harsh north of England climate. But having little money he was unable to update his winter wardrobe, so the running also kept him warm.

On his regular runs he would come across some local children playing football who he would stop and join in with, and so considered himself to be one of the first players to promote football in the community.

WORLD'S FIRST BLACK PROFESSIONAL FOOTBALLER ARTHUR 'KWAME' WHARTON

Although the first black player from South Africa to play in England was Steve Mokone in 1956, the first recognised black professional footballer dated way back to 1889. Arthur 'Kwame' Wharton (1865-1930) was born in Jamestown, Gold Coast (now Ghana), his mother was of Ghanaian royalty while his father was a missionary of Scottish and African descent.

As well as football, Arthur was an all-round sportsman who became the first sprinter to run 100 yards in 10 seconds in authentic championship conditions. His groundbreaking run was at Stamford Bridge on 3 July 1886. He was therefore recognised as being the world's first official fastest man when his 10 second run was ratified as being the first official record for that distance. His new world record would stand for over 30 years.

Along with his athletics, Arthur had a passion for football and joined Darlington FC as an amateur in the 1885-86 season, although surprisingly with the advantage of his tremendous speed he decided to be a goalkeeper. He made such an early impression that he was selected for the prestigious Newcastle and District team and was described as 'magnificent', 'invincible' and 'superb'. The Football League didn't start until 1888 so up until then the FA Cup was the main competition, along with district and county matches. After some good performances for Darlington, he was signed by Preston North End as an amateur, and was part of the team that reached the FA Cup semi-finals in 1886-87. Although he was receiving some support in the press, there was also an amount of blatant racism in some of the articles, with one such article being printed in one of the most popular sports papers at the time, the *Athletic Journal*:

"Good judges say that if Wharton keeps goal for the [Preston] North End in their English Cup tie the odds will be considerably lengthened against them. I am of the same opinion...Is the darkie's pate too thick for it to dawn upon him that between the posts is no place for a skylark? By some it's called coolness - bosh!"

Arthur didn't let such ignorance hold him back and he was part of the 'invincibles' Preston team that reached the FA Cup semi-finals in 1886-87, losing out to West Bromwich Albion 3-1. Arthur left Preston in 1888 to concentrate on his running, leaving a team that would go on to win the inaugural league championship in 1888-89, a season in which they went the whole 22 game season unbeaten (won 18, drew 4) also winning the FA Cup.

Football became a professional sport in the summer of 1885, and although Arthur had allegedly been receiving payments from Preston, it wasn't until 1889 that he signed a professional contract for Rotherham Town, making history by becoming the first black professional footballer.

Rotherham played in the Midland League and in his for years at the club they won the league on two consecutive occasions (1890-91 and 1891-92).

In 1894 Arthur signed for Sheffield United in Division One as understudy to regular first-team goalkeeper William "Fatty" Foulkes.

Photo: William 'Fatty' Foulkes

Arthur played in three first team games for Sheffield United in the First Division in the 1894-95 season, against Sunderland, Leicester Fosse and Linfield rendering him the first black/mixed race player in the world to play in the English top flight. In 1895, he left Sheffield and signed for Stalybridge Rovers but after falling out with the management he moved to Ashton North End in 1897.

When Ashton went bankrupt in 1899, Arthur returned to Stalybridge Rovers, before seeing out his career playing for Stockport County in the Second Division in 1901-02. Although predominantly a goalkeeper Arthur would, if needed, feature as an outfield player using his exceptional speed as a winger. In the football closed season Arthur's athletic skills were further used when he played professional cricket for Stalybridge Cricket Club, and on retiring from professional football in 1902 he continued playing cricket and running well into his fifties.

Arthur was seen as a unique figurehead who rose above the adversity and racism he faced in everyday life to be a professional sportsman. In later life he worked as a haulage worker and developed a problem with alcohol addiction, he died penniless aged 65 in December 1930.

He was buried in an unmarked grave in Edlington cemetery, but in 1997 he was given a headstone in recognition of his achievements by the Football Unites Racism Divides (FURD) organisation.

In 2012, a small statue of Arthur was presented to FIFA President, Sepp Blatter at the headquarters of FIFA where it is on permanent display.

On 16 October 2014, a 16-foot permanent memorial statue honouring Arthur was unveiled in the centre of the St. George's Cross in the memorial garden at the entrance to the National Football Centre in Staffordshire.

Photo: Arthur Wharton statue at St. George’s Park

WILLIE CLARKE – THE FIRST NON-WHITE GOALSCORER

William Gibb Clarke (1878-1949) was born in Mauchline, Ayrshire on 3 March, 1878. His mother, Jemima, was from Kilmarnock while his father, Alexander, was originally from British Guiana (now Guyana) having been sent to Scotland to complete his education.

Known as Willie he started playing football in Glasgow and was selected for his one and only cap for Scotland Juniors in an international match against Ireland in a 3-1 win on 29 March 1897, which made him the second black player to play for Scotland (after Andrew Watson).

After continuing to impress with his ability and aptitude, between 1897 and 1900 he turned professional with Third Lanark, Arthurlie and East Stirlingshire before moving south in August 1900 to join Southern League Bristol Rovers, becoming their first black player.

After playing in twenty games and impressing at Bristol, Willie was signed by first division Aston Villa who had previously won back-to-back championships in 1898-99 and 1899-00. Willie, who was also Aston Villa's first black player, created history by being the first non-white player to score in the English First Division.

While playing outside-right in a 3-2 win at Everton on Christmas Day 1901, Willie scored an historic goal that guaranteed him a place in history as the first non-white goalscorer. He made sixteen appearances for Villa in the 1901-02 season as they finished eighth out of eighteen in the league.

Willie stayed stay at Villa until 1905 adding a further 19 appearances and four goals to his tally before he was transferred to Bradford City.

Bradford were only one of two teams (the other being Chelsea) to join the Football League without having ever played a competitive game (they replaced Doncaster Rovers).

Willie spent four years at Bradford scoring 15 goals in 92 appearances (including Bradford's first ever goal in the first division). While at Bradford he helped them win the Second Division and promotion in 1907-08. His last professional team was Lincoln City, where he moved to from Bradford in 1909, playing 35 games and scoring one goal over two seasons. Willie finished his football career in 1912 after a season at Croydon Common. With the outbreak of World War I, he was one of the first to sign up to the Army in August 1914 only two weeks after the Great War broke out. He married his second wife Annie 'Nancy' Emeline in South Beddington during the war, on 25th October 1914, celebrating the birth of their first child, Richard, in September 1915.

He initially served as a Private in the Middlesex Regiment, before moving regiments to become a Sapper in the Royal Engineers. Willie served with distinction in the War and was awarded the 1914 Star, Victory Medal and the British War Medal.

Following the end of the war in 1918 he moved to Tunbridge Wells in Kent with his wife and they had a further five children; Raymond, Douglas, Donald, Bernard and June.

Willie returned to work as an upholsterer, the trade he had learned in Glasgow before his professional football career had started.

As a war hero and the first non-white goalscorer in history Willie deserves his place in history as a trailblazer.

He died in January 1949, aged 70, and was survived by Nancy, who passed away 20 years later.

Photo: Willie Clarke (front row, first left) in the Bradford City team which had won promotion in 1907-1908 and was ready to embark on their Division One campaign in 1908-09.

ALBERT'S INTRODUCTION TO ELLAND ROAD

Leeds United's stadium at Elland Road came into operation when the owners of the the Old Peacock pub, Bentleys Brewery, levelled the meadow opposite the pub and laid out a playing field, later known as The Old Peacock Ground. The pitch was used privately by the pub, and was also used by rugby players from Leeds Athletic Rugby Football Club.

Holbeck Rugby Club purchased the ground in 1897 and built the first stand which was ready for the 1898-99 season. In the early years, the venue was mainly used for rugby, although it also played host to football matches, including Leeds Woodville in the 1902/03 season.

In 1904, Holbeck Rugby Club were wound up and the newly formed Leeds City F.C initially leased the ground before eventually purchasing it for £4,500. Leeds City bought additional land around the ground and new stands were built. During World War I the ground was used for military parades and for shooting practice. Elland Road has always been Leeds United's home ground from their beginning in 1919 when United rose from the ashes of the disgraced Leeds City F.C. Leeds City had faced sanctions for paying its players during wartime (WWI) and was dissolved when the club's directors failed to co-operate with an FA inquiry. Leeds United took over Elland Road and entered the Second Division of the Football League in 1920. Behind the stadiums West Stand stood the football pitches of Fullerton Park, where Leeds would train right up until the late 1990s.

It was here that Albert got his first taste of English football.

A group of intrigued Leeds players had gathered to 'test' the new addition from South Africa. Albert recalls his feelings:

"It was incredible really. In South Africa, as a black man, I wasn't able to speak or look at a white person, now here I was, Albert Johanneson, being treated as an equal. As if that wasn't confusing enough, the weather completely threw me! I had never before seen snow, let alone ice on the ground. This was a whole new world for me, a new start, a new opportunity, a chance to make something of my life. I desperately wanted to succeed and do well not only for me, but for everyone back in South Africa. I fell in love with Leeds United."

After watching Albert play, Leeds coach Les Cocker said of him: "Albert was incredible, he would spin, turn and leave defenders ten yards behind in the blink of an eye."

Photo: Albert in his early days at Leeds

GERRY FRANCIS

LEEDS UNITED'S FIRST BLACK PLAYER

Gerry Francis was the second black player from South Africa to come to England to try to carve out a career in professional football. It is assumed by many that Albert Johanneson was the first black player to play for Leeds, but Gerry is in fact the first. Originally from Johannesburg, Gerry who was a shoe repairer in South Africa was the son of African and Asian parents, he was classed as mixed race and played for Blackpool Coloured FC in the mixed race league. He said he was due to go over to England with fellow South African Steve Mokone but he couldn't travel with him because he was delayed while waiting for his passport to be approved.

Gerry said his mum was delighted with him going to England, she said to him: "It's about time you did something with your life." Gerry said she thought that what he was doing was good for the country: "So everyone could see we weren't as stupid as the whites made us out to be." Gerry paid his own way to England at the end of the 1956-57 season and was trialled at Leeds before signing professional for them in July 1957, making him the first black player to represent Leeds United as well as the first black South African to play in the First Division. The Leeds manager at the time was Raich Carter who gave right-winger Gerry his debut in a Division 1 home game against Birmingham City on 30 November 1957 in front of a crowd of 21,358. The game finished in a 1-1 draw.

Leeds had been promoted under Carter in the 1956/57 season and the following year in their first season in the top flight (after a nine-year absence) they finished a credible eighth with the legendary John Charles scoring 38 goals. When Charles moved to Juventus in the summer Leeds struggled the following season without his goals.

Gerry made his debut but that was the only appearance in a disappointing season in which Leeds finished a lowly 17th. Gerry felt his lack of appearances under Carter was racially motivated. He said on the situation: "I didn't feel I was treated the same, inferior players got in first. So I started to get mad. I approached Raich Carter but I could see I wasn't going to get an answer from him. He was only doing what the top men, the owners, were telling him to do. One of them didn't like me in the team. I think being black was the problem. There weren't many clubs with two non-white players. I think some people didn't like that."

When Carter's contract wasn't renewed the new caretaker manager Willis Edwards still didn't pick Gerry. Edwards was replaced in December 1958 by Bill Lambton, who although signing future Leeds legends Don Revie and Billy Bremner only lasted as manager for four months, in which time he also overlooked Gerry. While at Leeds Gerry shared digs with Billy Bremner but when Albert Johanneson arrived he said Albert was the one he became closest to as: "Albert needed him the most."

It wasn't be until 9 September 1959 that Gerry would be recalled to the first team by the new manager Jack Taylor, playing in a team alongside the legendary Jack Charlton and Don Revie. The match was away at arch rivals Manchester United and in front of a crowd of 48,619, but Leeds suffered an ignominious 6-0 defeat. Gerry didn't play in the following three fixtures, but he did return on 10 October 1959 when he scored his first goal in a 3-3 draw at home to Everton in front of a 19,122 crowd. He retained his place the following week in the game away at Blackpool, when he scored again in another 3-3 draw in front of a crowd of 22,301. He continued his run in the side for the following three fixtures, a 1-0 home defeat to Blackburn in front of 17,159, a 1-1 draw away at Bolton in front of 20,183 and a 3-2 home win over Arsenal in front of a crowd of 21,617. Gerry was then in out of the side until the end of the season, finishing off in the side for the last game of the season on 30 April in a 1-0 win at home to Nottingham Forest in front of a disappointing crowd of 11,699. The crowd reflected the fact that Leeds had already been relegated before the final game after finishing second from bottom with 34 points from 42 games, 4 points above bottom placed Luton Town.

Gerry played in 12 games in the 1959/60 season scoring 3 goals.

Gerry didn't feature in the first game in Division 2 in the 1960-61 season, a 2-0 defeat to Liverpool in front of 43,041 fans, but he did play in the following four games. Leeds were struggling in their first season back in Division 2 and in March 1961 Jack Taylor was replaced as manager by Don Revie. Gerry played in Revie's first game in charge on 18 March 1961 in a 3-1 defeat away at Portsmouth in front of 16,230 fans. He played a further four games that season under Revie, but with the emerging influence of a young Billy Bremner and the exciting new signing of fellow South African, Albert Johanneson, Gerry's chances became limited. Gerry and Albert did play together once in the same team, in Albert's second appearance for Leeds in a 0-0 draw away at Stoke City on 15 April 1961 in front of a crowd of 7,130. This was the first time that two black players appeared together in a football league match. Gerry said of Albert: "He was very quiet to begin with, later he was more outgoing but when he first came, I took him in hand and showed him the ropes. He needed some help. It was hard for him, the same as it could be difficult for me at the start. I never mixed with white people because of apartheid and he didn't speak much English when he went to England. The two of us, we'd speak Africaans. People would say to us, 'What the hell are you two talking about?' And it was like our own secret language but I tried to teach Albert more English. I'd read to him and I'd translate to him. When we spoke he was a damn good guy to listen to. But he was a loner as well. The language was a barrier for him."

Leeds finished the disappointing 1961-62 season in front of their lowest league attendance since the war when just 6,975 turned up for a 2-2 draw with Scunthorpe United. Gerry was omitted from the team but Albert played. Revie knew he had a major task on his hands but set about it with fervour, changing the way players were paid by incentivising their pay as opposed to different pay for different players. Packages of up to £43 10s per player per week was generous for the early 1960s. The basic wage was increased to £20 per week, to be supplemented by a £5 appearance fee, a £4 win bonus and a complex sliding scale of incentives aligned to attendances above 20,000. To qualify for the full bonus of £14 10s, Leeds would have to draw a crowd of more than 31,000, an ambitious plan as it would need an increase of 18,000 above the previous year's average.

Gerry wouldn't be around to see the fruition of Revie's ambitions as he was transferred to York City (ironically where Albert would also move to nine years later) in October 1961. Gerry's last game for Leeds United was in a 2-1 defeat at home to Preston on 30 September 1961 in front of 9,360 fans. Albert said of Gerry leaving Leeds: "When Gerry left I felt more vulnerable than I had ever been at the club. Gerry was one of the few people who knew what it was like being a black footballer in a white country, I think his transfer affected me more than it did him."

Gerry played 16 games for York that season, scoring four goals before moving to Tonbridge where he said he had his happiest time as everyone was so friendly. Gerry married his wife, Francis, in 1962 and Albert was proud to be Best Man at their wedding. In 1971 Gerry and Francis migrated to Canada with their two children. They retired to the Canadian City of Mississauga near Toronto, and after leaving England, Gerry said he was sad to hear of Albert's demise. Saying:

"In our years together we lived cleanly and soberly. I never drank or smoked and Albert used to follow everything I did, so he didn't drink or smoke either. With him it all came later, I don't know what happened when I left." Gerry made the trip back to England in 1998 to visit Albert's grave. Gerry said of Albert: "I never wanted to believe he was having problems, you don't want to believe things like that. It was a shock to me." Looking back at his own time in England, Gerry had a different view to what Albert had on the racism they received.

Gerry said that he wouldn't let the name calling get to him.

"I didn't bother with anyone who called me names. The crowds would try to put you off that way, but in my first game in England in a reserve game at Blackpool, fellow South African Bill Perry was in the Blackpool line-up." Perry is best remembered for scoring the winning goal in the 1953 FA Cup Final in 92nd minute in a 4-3 win over Bolton Wanderers . Perry chatted with Gerry on the pitch before the game and lifted his arm up towards the crowd as a salute, the crowd in return gave him a big ovation, Gerry said: "It made me realise that everybody was everybody here."

Albert said of Gerry: "We got to know each other well, he was such a good human being and go out of his way to help anyone. Gerry would point me in the right direction. He introduced me to many different people in the city who he thought would be supportive of me, that's the type of man Gerry was."

A rare Leeds United team photo with both Gerry and Albert 1961-62

(Gerry – middle row far right, Albert middle row third player in)

ALBERT SIGNS FOR LEEDS UNITED

Albert recalled his first day at training as 'daunting' but he said fellow South African Gerry Francis met him with a 'huge hug and beaming smile'. Having no football boots of his own, Albert was issued a pair, but having not being used to boots, he said they were 'uncomfortable' like 'someone had bound his feet in rope'. Billy Bremner commented that Albert looked like he had lead diving boots on! Billy gave Albert advice on how to 'wear a boot in' and told him that he must never play in bare feet as it would ruin his career. Albert said he thought Billy was a pleasant young man and that he had given him a rousing chat that made him feel welcome. Gerry Francis confirmed to Albert that indeed Billy was one of the best people at the club.

Photo: Billy celebrating one of Albert's goals

Training with Billy was a different matter altogether though, Albert said the first time he came up against him in practice, Billy sent him flying through the air and crashing to the ground in the cold and muddy grass. As he came around, he heard the comments 'Welcome to Leeds' and 'Enjoy your Bremner mud bath'. Albert knew it was all light-hearted but he did make a note to himself to try and get on Billy's side in future sessions.

Having featured well in his first training session at Elland Road, Albert had been seen to 'pass' his test in front of his potential new team-mates. And so after a tough training session in the cold Yorkshire climate, with no favours given by the tough tackling defenders, Albert had withstood the physicality and had let his speed and skill shine through.

At first the change in the climate from the glorious sunshine of South Africa to the chill of northern England had affected Albert quite badly, he said: "One Monday in Leeds I did not want to get out of bed because it was so cold. I had a trial and they took me off because it was too cold. I thought I was finished." But he wasn't going to let the cold scupper his chance and he was determined to be as committed as he possibly could in fighting for a professional contract.

Although Albert was lacking in self-confidence he continued to impress in training, with *The Yorkshire Evening Post* giving a report on his practise sessions: "His superior skills on the training ground 'demoralised' the other players who were consistently 'run into the ground' by the South African."

Albert was described as 'Fast as a Yorkshire Whippet with feet like a ballroom dancer.' And as well as the 'Hurry Hurry' tag he was often referred to as 'The Black Flash' due to his electric speed.

With the glowing newspaper reports, he was further buoyed after a conversation he had with Jack Taylor shortly after Albert had watched his first Leeds game, a 2-0 defeat at Sheffield Wednesday. Taylor told Albert that although he had some good 'solid players', he said some were not up to the challenge and he needed to bring in some fresh new young players in, and that he wanted Albert to be one of those players who could meet his standards. He told Albert to be himself and he would earn respect. Albert appreciated the talk with Taylor saying: "No one had ever spoken to me in such a way, from that moment on I had nothing but the utmost respect for Mr Taylor." Unfortunately, as is the way in life, this was the last conversation Albert had with Taylor as results and Leeds position in the league were so poor that Taylor resigned (with a nudge) on 13 March 1961. Albert said of Taylor's resignation: "The atmosphere at the house and at the club was dreadful, everyone felt insecure about their future."

Albert, not knowing that Don Revie was to be appointed as manager approached him for advice on his situation. Although he said Revie 'hadn't been over friendly' with him since he arrived and 'standoffish', he asked Albert if he really wanted to play for Leeds, and if his heart was at Leeds United. Albert said it was and that he would do anything to sign professional terms for Leeds. Revie's reply was to say: "Well, then, wait until the new manager comes in and see what happens."

Don Revie was appointed as player/manager to replace Taylor a few days later in March 1961. Revie had been an outstanding player at Manchester City and Sunderland before signing for Leeds in November 1958, winning the Football Writers Association Footballer of the Year in 1954-55 while at Man City. As a player Revie had an 18-year professional career from 1944-1962, playing for England six times in the 1955-56 season scoring four international goals. Revie had also been one of many signatories in a letter to *The Times* on 17 July 1958 opposing 'the policy of apartheid' in international sport and defending 'the principle of racial equality which is embodied in the Declaration of the Olympic Games'.

Photo: Don Revie is welcomed as manager by Derek Mayers, Colin Grainger, Peter McConnell, Gerry Francis, Grenville Hair, Jack Charlton and Jimmy Ashall

Revie took over a Leeds side that was in a perilous position. The town was predominantly rugby league orientated and they were £250,000 in debt. Leeds needed crowds of around 30,000 just to break-even but were averaging attendances of only 18,000 and at some games only 13,000 were turning up. With relegation to the third division a distinct possibility, Harry Reynolds a self-made down-to-earth retired businessman took over the role of chairman from Sam Bolton. In his tenure as Chairman, Reynolds changed the atmosphere at the club in an attempt to make everyone feel important, whether it was player's wives, ground staff cleaners or tea ladies, he treated everyone with respect. He had total belief in Revie and despite the debt Leeds were in, if Revie wanted a player, Reynolds would try his utmost so that Revie would get his man. Revie and Reynolds formed a strong bond which would eventually be the key to Leeds United's future success. But first they had to stop the directors from trying to offload Billy Bremner and Jack Charlton to finance the club. Reynolds provided £50,000 of finance to support the club and Leeds were thankfully able to hang on to their prized possessions.

Albert was still struggling to settle to life in England and sought solace in St Mary's Church in Beeston, he described himself as a devout Christian who enjoyed religion and wanted to find spiritual strength to help him through his trial period. He was warmly welcomed into the church and although he faced racist comments on the streets of Leeds, he said the two positives of his early days in Yorkshire was the unity of his Leeds United colleague's and the support from the church.

In the early days, Albert said he was still in turmoil, he didn't feel like he had anyone to talk to and didn't want anyone to think it was a weakness if he opened up. He wanted to prove himself as an equal, hoping that if he could prove himself good enough it would give credence to other black South African footballers back home that they could also be taken seriously.

In 1961 it was estimated that there were only 450 Africans in Leeds out of a population of over 715,000. He said the racism he faced was upsetting and soul destroying but he looked on the bright side by saying: "For every dozen or so rude people I encountered there was a further half dozen who were good, friendly and genuinely okay with me as a black man in a predominantly white country." Albert received supportive words from people within the club and was appreciative of advice from friend and one-club man, left-back Grenville Hair who played for Leeds from 1948-64 playing 443 games. Grenville said: "Albert, things will happen in football that really surprise you, nothing is straight forward, it's a tough world and only the fittest survive, especially at good clubs like this. Every time you get knocked back you need to learn from it and come back even stronger." Albert was thankful for the advice and took note. He was saddened to hear that when his playing career finished, Grenville who had just taken on the role of Bradford City manager, sadly died during a training session in March 1968 aged only 36.

Albert said after Revie was appointed as manager: "I believed my time at the club was over, but I carried on training and working hard to impress everyone at the club, but Revie or 'Boss' as he wanted to be called never spoke a word to me or even glanced at me. I felt anonymous." He continued: "Then, totally out of the blue, Syd Owen came to the house at Noster Hill and asked to speak with me. I knew it was decision time. I was to go to the ground for a meeting with the boss. I was sure there was no way he would offer me a contract. I was close to tears when I entered his office."

But Revie had other ideas, he had been able to monitor Albert closely having trained with him on a daily basis, and although he had concerns he had been suitably impressed with Albert's application and of course his amazing speed.

After asking Albert how he thought he had done over his three month trial, Revie said: "I have some contradictory reports about you, and they concern me. Some people say you glide past players with ease and you can do almost anything with a football. Others tell me that you don't like getting stuck in when it matters. I've been watching you in training and in your extra work with Les (Leeds trainer Les Cocker), sometimes you amaze me, your skill and pace is breathtaking, your balance is majestic and the way you can leave players like Billy Bremner in your wake is bewildering. Everyone I speak to tells me you are a very nice man. I don't like you being a nice and polite man, I need you to toughen up Albert, don't be afraid to get stuck in where it hurts, don't give up the ball easily, fight for it, shout for it when you don't have it. What's your feelings on that? How do you feel, can you do that for me?" Albert told him that he could and would do as he asks. "Right then" said Revie, "Albert Louis Johanneson, I want you here as part of my Leeds United. You have got yourself a contract, it's of extreme importance for both you and me at this moment, because I am making you my first signing for this football club." Albert was both shocked and delighted.

Revie went on: "I want to see passion in your game, the grit and determination side of your game has to be in there, let it emerge, I want you to fight for the cause of Leeds United, I want you to give everything and if necessary, be prepared to die for the sake of this football club's success. I would do that, so I expect you to do it too. Don't let me down Albert, if you do, you'll be on the first plane back to South Africa. I'm taking a huge gamble on you delivering, so welcome to Leeds United, this is my Leeds United and you'll answer to me only do you understand that? Albert nodded his agreement. Revie smiled and said: "Well done lad, now stop snivelling and get yourself back up the hill."

Albert later confessed that he had burst into tears at the news and was sobbing uncontrollably. Revie finished by telling him that now he was a professional footballer he was to go out and get himself a decent suit, shirt and tie, and had to: "start acting like a man and not the shoeshine boy you think you are, people will look up to you Albert so act accordingly." Albert left Elland Road elated although a little sad that he wasn't able to share the moment with his family back in South Africa.

Although still extremely shy, Albert had endeared himself to the Leeds United 'family' that Don Revie was in the process of building. He had high hopes of settling in a country where he could live out his dream and earn enough money to provide for his family, away from the violence and prejudice they had openly faced in South Africa.

Both Jack Taylor and then Revie had seen the potential in Albert throughout his three month trial at Leeds and Les Cocker would champion Albert's style of play.

Albert was the catalyst for Don Revie's Leeds United to rise to the top of English and European football when he became Revie's very first signing as a manager when he signed his professional contract on 5 April 1961. The terms of his contract was that he would earn approximately £15 a week (approx. worth £250 in 2022).

With little fuss, and sporting a dashing Clark Gable style moustache, Albert signed his contract under the watchful eye of the fatherly figures of Chairman Harry Reynolds and manager Don Revie, with the signing being witnessed by Leeds first black professional footballer and good friend, Gerry Francis.

Albert was a proud man and had achieved what he had set out to do after leaving South Africa, but he knew he still had a long way to go. But for now he couldn't wait to tell his family back home that he had signed his first professional contract.

Photo: Gerry Francis, Don Revie and Chairman Harry Reynolds watch on as Albert signs his first professional contract

In order to turn them into winners, Revie's intention was to completely change the mind-set at Leeds.

Despite Albert's doubts about his own talent and impact, Revie said of signing Albert: "I saw in Albert a bright talent that I could develop. He was quick exciting and different in every way, and other players were enthused by his potential. He was a player I couldn't let go, he was already creating attention elsewhere with other clubs monitoring his situation and I saw it as a test of my own ambition and expectations."

Revie acknowledged there was a demand for Albert when he said: "Albert didn't know it but two first division teams were watching his situation very closely, if I had allowed him to leave us, he would have been snapped up by someone else in a higher division. Had he known of the interest then he may well have spoken to those clubs and been offered better terms. I know he would have gone and we would have lost out. That speaks volumes for his ability, but also about my desire not to lose out on anything. I was a winner with a winning attitude. I wanted winners at my club. Albert was my first signing for Leeds United, I had doubts about him, and to be truthful, it was Les Cocker who finally persuaded me that Albert was of sufficient quality to represent the club. Les said that Albert would light up every football pitch in Europe with his blistering pace and ball control. In signing him I was helping my own reputation as a manager with real vision, and a new international image for the football club. Albert could do things with a football that most players I knew could only dream of."

When Albert later found out about other clubs interest in him he said it would have made no difference to his decision to sign. He was committed to Leeds and had started to recognise it as home.

Photo: Les Cocker and Don Revie on England duty.

As Albert began to settle into his new life in Leeds and started to venture out more with his new Leeds team mates. He rekindled his love of music and dancing, saying: "I remember going to dances at places like Armley, Bramley and Pudsey baths and to different town halls. It was good to be able to mix and socialise in such places, we all had a common purpose, to dance and enjoy ourselves and it felt very good." He said of dancing: "It's like physical poetry, gliding gracefully is a real skill, it was very much part of how I saw my football skills, like a dancer, gliding past challenges, turning, twisting, fast and then slow, calm and then erratic. I was always singing or humming to myself."

Leeds United legendary captain 'King' Billy Bremner who although young himself would take Albert under his wing and said of Albert's signing: "When he joined Leeds the rest of the team stood open-mouthed, drooling over his trickery. He was a bloody excellent player and had so much pace and strength, he was a great athlete. He was incredible, he would spin, turn and leave defenders ten yards behind in the blink of an eye."

Photo: Albert and the protective Billy Bremner

BRITISH WAR HERO - WALTER DANIEL JOHN TULL

The story of Walter Tull deserves to be retold not only for his trailblazing football exploits but for his remarkable heroics fighting in World War I.

Walter Daniel John Tull (1888-1918) was the first black outfield player to feature regularly in English football's top flight, and only the second black player to play professional football in Britain.

He was brought up in a Children's Home and Orphanage after the death of his mother when he was only seven. Both Walter and his brother were admitted to the Dr Stephenson's Children's Home in Bethnal Green, London. Neither of the boys would let their early childhood difficulties impede their way in life, Edward would reportedly go on to become the first black professional dentist when he qualified in 1912, while Walter became a professional footballer and heroic soldier.

Walter began his football career at east London amateur side Clapton, where he would win the London Senior Cup, the FA Amateur Cup and the London County Amateur Cup during the 1908-09 season. After impressing at Clapton, Walter was invited by Tottenham on their pre-season tour to South America in the summer of 1909. After showing great promise, Walter was offered a professional contract with Tottenham which he duly signed in time for the 1909-10 season. He made his debut in the opening game of the First Division season, losing 3-1 at Sunderland on 1 September 1909 in front of 10,000 spectators.

Photo: Walter with his brother Edward Tull-Warnock who became the first black dentist in the UK

Although winning praise for his on the field performances, Walter still faced a substantial amount of prejudice and racial abuse from the footballing terraces. Walter went on to play a further 9 games for Tottenham (scoring two goals) before he signed for Northampton Town under the management of the legendary Herbert Chapman in 1911.

After Chapman left to manage Leeds, Walter remained at Northampton becoming an important and popular player, going on to play 110 games for them over 3 seasons, scoring 9 goals.

With the outbreak of First World War in 1914, Walter joined the British Army in December 1914 and after returning from an officer's training course he signed for Glasgow Rangers on 2 February 1915. Unfortunately, he never managed to make an appearance for Rangers as he was shipped overseas to fight in the War.

Walter was promoted to sergeant by the end of 1915, but was sent back to Britain in May 1916 after suffering from what was recorded on his medical records as 'acute mania', renamed shellshock soon after.

As soon as he recovered, Walter returned to the battlefields and with his 'gallantry and coolness' in battle he was commissioned as a lieutenant in May 1917, and in doing so he became the first British-born black army officer and the first black officer to lead white British troops into battle.

Walter's rise was all the more remarkable due to the fact that there was a military rule excluding 'negroes' from exercising actual command.

Walter led his troops with distinction but was sadly killed in action near the village of Favreuil in the Pas-de-Calais in France on 25 March 1918 during the First Battle of Bapaume.

In 2014, to recognise the centenary of World War I, Walter was honoured with his own £5 coin. The Walter Tull commemorative coin, features Arthur's portrait as an officer with a backdrop of infantry soldiers going 'over the top'. The coin is one of a set of six £5 coins to remember the sacrifice made by so many during the war, and to recognise Arthur as a true British hero who overcame prejudices to excel in both his sporting career, and in his defence of his country. On Armed Forces' Day in 2018, 127 MPs from six different parties signed a letter to the Prime Minister requesting that Walter be honoured with the Military Cross posthumously serving. Tottenham MP David Lammy said: "Walter Tull is a true British hero and he embodies everything that makes me so proud to be British. I think that everybody in our country should know Walter's story."

"ME OLD FLOWER" CHARLIE WILLIAMS

Charlie Williams was one of Britain's first black professional footballers in the late 1940/50s who would go on to become one of the country's greatest comedians.

Charlie's father had moved from the West Indies to settle in Yorkshire, working as a coalminer and marrying a South Yorkshire lass, Doris Cook. Charlie was a product of their union and was born in Barnsley in December 1928.

Charlie was only eleven years-old when World War II broke out and with little education he left school without any qualifications when he was only fourteen.

With the War depleting coal rations there was a great demand for coal but not enough miners. Consequently the government introduced conscription and directed ten percent of the conscript's to work in the mines instead of the armed forces. Charlie became one of the 'Bevin Boys' (named after Ernest Bevin, the Minister of Labour) and began working long hours down the pit at Monkton Colliery.

Charlie who described himself as 'half-caste' (a term used for children of mixed marriages) never let the prejudice he faced affect him. With a great personality and natural humour he could easily diffuse any negativity. When he was asked by a misguided group if he was enjoying himself in England, he jovially replied in his broad Yorkshire accent: "I certainly am, my old love."

Charlie worked down the mines leading the pit ponies up and down the coal faces with tubs of coal attached to them. The work was long and hard, but Charlie had a way out of the drudgery through his footballing ability.

Described as an uncompromising, athletic centre-half, while he was playing for the local colliery football team, he was spotted by Leeds United and offered trials with them. Charlie was nineteen at the time and spent four months on trial at Leeds, but as it was just after the war (1947), money was tight, and Leeds would only offer Charlie amateur terms.

Charlie declined the offer and further trials with Notts County, York City and Doncaster Rovers were more fruitful, leading to a semi-professional contract at Doncaster Rovers for the 1947-48 season. After impressing in the reserves, Charlie signed a full professional contract in 1948, enabling him to leave the toil of the pits and become one of the first black professional footballers.

Charlie thrived in his new career and although he would hear the regular taunt of 'Get back to Africa' he said the comradery of fellow players and the support from the majority of fans made it easy for him to ignore.

Initially Charlie played the majority of his first few seasons at Doncaster in the reserves, until he became a first team regular in 1953. He laughed as he recalled that in his early appearances in the first-team, as soon as he entered the field of play the away crowd would let out a huge gasp at seeing a player of colour on the pitch.

Charlie said he did receive a lot of abuse in relation to his colour, but he found it easier to turn the other cheek than confront the abusers. He recalled: "We'd call each other names during the match but afterwards you would shake hands and be friends. Some fans would even come up and say sorry." One of his team-mates lauded his ability to bear no malice towards his aggressors by saying: "He never took the bait and kept his dignity on and off the pitch. He would just channel the negative energy and show more determination."

Charlie had been an athlete from a young age and was supremely fit. He would do cross-country runs on his own straight after training, he avoided alcohol and followed a healthy diet. By his own admission he was not the most skilful of players, but what he lacked in finesse he made up for in speed and athleticism. He said of his style of play: "The ball might have gone past me, and sometimes the player, but never both at the same time."

Ray Singleton played against Charlie early in his career and said of him: "He would kick you to death then laugh. He was a good sportsman and never bore a grudge, but then he wasn't the one usually injured. He had a nice way with him and would often sit with you telling jokes as the physio tried to help you walk again."

Charlie met the delightfully named Audrey Crump in the 1953-54 season and although there was considerable opposition to mixed marriages, they were married in 1957. Charlie by now was a regular in the Doncaster first-team, and would eventually go on to play 151 games with Doncaster in Division two and three. At thirty-two and slowing down he moved to Skegness Town in the Midland League.

Skegness were managed by the famous manager George Rayner who had taken Sweden to third place in the 1954 World Cup Finals and followed that up by reaching the final in 1958, losing out to a Pele inspired Brazil 5-2. Rayner offered Charlie a contract worth £15 per week and a part-time job delivering Skegness confectionary rock for the Club President's company. Aligned with subsidised rent on a house, Charlie was on a better deal than at Doncaster.

After a couple of successful seasons at Skegness (gaining promotion in one) Charlie moved on to Denaby Main FC in Doncaster. While at Denaby Charlie received an offer to go to Sydney Prague FC in Australia on a lucrative two-year contract where his old friend and playing colleague Alick Jeffrey was playing. Charlie accepted the offer and the local news ran features on his imminent departure to Australia.

Having put all his affairs in order, including leasing his home for the two year period while he would be away, Charlie sent his application and passport to Australia House to enable him to gain a work permit to cover his time in Australia. Unfortunately with his passport revealing he was black, the offer of the contract was suddenly withdrawn.

The withdrawal of the contract had no explanation other than the colour of his skin, raising allegations of racial prejudice against the Australian government. The Barnsley Chronicle championed Charlie's story and it wasn't long before the national press became involved. Newspaper headlines claiming the action was racially motivated put pressure on the Australian Embassy to clarify the position. The story escalated with the Australian press getting involved, and from what was originally seen as a simple contract withdrawal, escalated into an international condemnation of Australian government policy.

Robert Menzies the Australian Prime Minister issued a statement to try and calm the situation by saying that there was no colour bar in Australia. Not long after the Prime Minister's statement the contract offer to Charlie was re-issued, but after careful thought and a heavy heart Charlie declined the offer. His reasoning was that the offer had been made under duress and therefore would distract from his ability to do the job effectively and undermine his position. Charlie's decision was a difficult and courageous one to make as he was fully aware that his footballing career was coming to an end and there was no other form of employment lined up.

Charlie had always had a way of performing about him, often singing 'crooner' style in local clubs. Although he was making a semi-professional living from singing, it was the comedy side of showbiz which he began to incorporate more and more into his singing performances that would lead to national stardom for Charlie.

After a soul destroying spell on the dole, Charlie did the rounds in the tough working men's clubs of the industrial north. Over time he proved to be a big hit with his brand of self-depreciating humour in his broad

Yorkshire accent. Success came in 1970 when he was invited to appear in the Yorkshire clubland command performance, which was followed by *The Comedians,* a popular show which gave a stage to nightclub and working men's club comedians of the era, on national television. Charlie followed his ground-breaking football career by becoming the first black British stand-up comic to experience mainstream success.

His humour struck a chord with the British public and in 1972 he played a six-month season at the London Palladium and had his own Granada television show, '*It's Charlie Williams*.' Other successes followed. His life story was told on the very popular national ITV show *This is Your Life*, and he appeared in the Royal Variety Command Performance (both in 1972). The following year he had his own *Charlie Williams Show* on the BBC, and he hosted ATV's game show *The Golden Shot* from 1973 to 1974. Charlie often poked fun at his colour, dabbling with race issues with a lot of his jokes being at his own expense. Although later castigated by 'new wave' black comedians over his 'darkie jokes' such as 'I've been left in the oven too long' or 'I'm perspiring a lot, I'm leaking chocolate' he said when he retired in 1995: "I don't have any regrets, I told jokes that I thought would suit the audience."

Charlie was a legend and should be remembered as a true trailblazer for his careers in both football and entertainment.

His work was recognised in 1999 when he received an MBE for his charity work, and in 2004 he was voted Doncaster Rovers "all-time cult hero". Charlie died on the 2nd September 2006 having suffered from Parkinson's disease and dementia.

ALBERT MAKES HIS DEBUT

Photo: Albert showing his skills on Fullerton Park.

After signing his first professional contract, Albert celebrated by visiting St Mary's church to give prayer to those who had supported him in his struggle to be accepted.

Following the contract signing on Wednesday 5 April 1961, he faced several particularly tough training sessions and on the Friday he felt there was a lot of focus on him. After training he checked the team sheet for the second team game but his name was missing, he was disappointed and assumed that he had been left out of the team. Dejected he went back to his digs to enjoy one of Mrs Wineley's home made lunches.

During lunch there was a phone call for him. It was Les Cocker wishing him good luck for his first team debut against Swansea Town the following day! Albert said he couldn't believe it and he was shaking with excitement. He received a hug from Mrs Wineley who said she was very proud of him and that he should be proud for all his hard work.

With substitutes not yet introduced by the Football League, Albert went straight into the side three days after he had signed his contract on Saturday 8 April 1961 in a Division 2 league fixture against Swansea Town (later City) in a team featuring, Billy Bremner, Jack Charlton and ex Manchester United player, Freddie Goodwin. Albert said that Freddie and Billy looked after him before the game, with Freddie telling him that he should be aware of the away fans, saying 'they'll crucify you if you let them'. He added that 'they hated everyone on the opposition team and it wasn't personal so rip them apart and let football be your voice.'

The Leeds team for Albert's debut in front of 11,862 fans was:

1. Alan Humphreys
2. Grenville Hair
3. John Kilford
4. Eric Smith (Scottish)
5. Freddie Goodwin
6. Peter McConnell
7. Peter Fitzgerald
8. Billy Bremner
9. Jack Charlton
10. Noel Peyton
11. Albert Johanneson

With fellow black player Gerry Francis not playing, Albert felt like he was the only black person in the ground (and probably was). As he warmed up he heard the appalling sound of a small group of away supporters making monkey noises as well as calling him 'darkie' and throwing bananas on to the pitch.

Albert remembers Billy Bremner marching up to the away supporters and confronting them, asking what their problem was. Although at first, he was given abuse the small group backed off when other players gathered around Billy. Billy lectured them to grow up and shut up stating that people were here to watch football not hurt people.

Photo: A Typical 1960s All White Football Crowd

Albert still heard abusive calls throughout the game, but Billy had inspired him before the game: "Let's shut their big stupid mouths, let's do it Albert, let's bloody do it." Albert appreciated Billy's support, feeling fired up he said that Billy was a true leader.

Albert said he was receiving abuse on the field as well as from the terraces. After avoiding a tackle which he was convinced was an attempt to hurt him rather than win the ball, from his sprawled position on the floor his embarrassed opponent said 'You black twat, I'll break your neck for this'.

But with the roar of the home fans behind him, Albert refused to let the abuse affect his game and put in an impressive performance, setting up a goal for centre forward for the day, Jack Charlton.

After the goal, Albert said: "I didn't know what to do, I was reluctant to celebrate in front of all the white men in the crowd, I was worried it may cause a riot, so I stood still and looked on. I felt numb and closed my eyes and thanked God for helping me. To my amazement, when I looked up, Jack and several other Leeds players were sprinting towards me with their arms held wide open. I was emotionally lost, I wanted to cry with happiness."

The report in the newspaper on the goal read:

'A perfect left cross almost ended this battle after 75 seconds. The Leeds left winger, Johanneson, left Swansea's defence dizzy with his first attack. He flashed down the left flank past three Welsh tackles and whipped the ball on to the talented head of centre forward Jackie Charlton. It zipped into the net like a bullet and Swansea with only one defeat in their last thirteen games were thrown out of gear.'

A draw at home against a tough Swansea team was a good start, with a win being in their grasp but Jack Charlton squandered his chance of a hat-trick when he missed a penalty late on. Although Albert was disappointed at not to have won the game, he was satisfied with his own performance feeling that he hadn't let anyone down.

After the game Billy Bremner asked Albert why he didn't get in the bath, Albert replied: "I didn't think other players would want to share a bath with a black man." The Leeds players were having none of it and collectively grabbed Albert and threw him into the bath. He said he was shaking with excitement: "I felt so happy and content. A few minutes earlier the football supporters of Swansea had made me feel very different, hated. Now I felt I was amongst my own kind of people, they were all white, and they couldn't see, or at least didn't show, that they saw me as black and different."

Albert had made a great start to his new Leeds career and impressed with his speed and grace. *The Yorkshire Post* boosted his confidence further when their report read: 'he got off to a most promising start. He has a good left foot, a great body swerve and looked very good when he came infield.'

After the game, Albert confessed to being overcome with emotion and having a little cry, but he was buoyed with the support the players gave him.

After his debut he began to receive more attention and adulation with the press taking note of his exciting promise.

But Albert said the most satisfaction he got was from the local kids calling for him at Noster Hill to see if he would play out and show them some tricks!

Photo: Albert in action on his debut against Swansea 8 April 1961

After his performance, Don Revie gave Albert the thumbs up and offered him some advice, he said: "You are settling in well Albert, everyone has been impressed by the way you conduct yourself. I don't think I have seen anyone quicker than you when you set off down the wing, your crossing and ball delivery is exceptional. Having said that, I would like to see you being a bit more ruthless and greedy, instead of getting to the byline and crossing, try getting into the penalty area and try to go for goal yourself. As you know, centre forwards aren't as quick as wingers and often take time to create and find the right goalscoring position inside the penalty area. I can see this may frustrate you, having to wait for your colleagues to catch up with you, so when that happens, just go for goal yourself. In training you are the same, don't be frightened to shoot, just let loose Albert, give the opposition goalkeeper and defenders something to worry about. Even if you are 25 yards out, if you think you can score, go for it."

FIRST BLACK PLAYER TO REPRESENT ENGLAND AT ANY LEVEL

There is a debate over who is recognised as the first black player to represent England at any level. There are nuances that seem to be taken into consideration in what constitutes a black player. In 1962 West Ham full-back John Charles (nicknamed Charlo) became the first black man (he was mixed race) to represent England when he made his debut for the England Under-18s side, but Benjamin Odeje (Boy Pele) is recognised by the FA as England's first black player when he was selected for England schoolboys as a 15-year-old, against Northern Ireland in front of 70,000 people at Wembley in March 1971. In total Ben played five times for England schoolboys, although there was controversy when he was mysteriously dropped and his story was highlighted in the local press.

ELL

Odeje is dropped by England—and Blackheath official resigns as protest storm grows

by TONY STENSON

CATFORD schoolmaster Don Paine has resigned after 25 years association with schoolboy football in protest over the shock dropping of Blackheath's Benny Odeje from the England international team.

Fifteen-year-old Odeje, from Childeric-rd., New Cross, was generally reckoned to be one of the best players on the field in his England Schools debut at Wembley on Saturday.

Yet he has been mysteriously left out for the next international later this month, and replaced by another coloured boy.

Paine, a tremendously hard-working official, has taken such a drastic step so that he will not embarrass the Blackheath FA with any future action he may take.

He intends to lead a campaign asking the English Schools FA for an explanation why 15-year-old Odeje, the first Nigerian to play for England, has been omitted.

ALREADY

It's understood that Paine, treasurer from the days when Blackheath operated as Lewisham, has already sent a letter to Schools FA authorities.

He says, "It's true I have tendered my resignation to the Blackheath FA because I feel so strongly about this. There has been a grave injustice

BENNY (centre) makes the nerve-racking walk from the tunnel.

BENJAMIN ODEJE

Following on with the confusion as to who qualifies as a black man in terms of representation of their country, initially the FA officially recognised Laurie Cunningham as the first black player to represent England at any level when he featured for England Under-21s in 1977.

However, in 2022 Charlton's Benjamin Odeje who was born in Nigeria was finally recognised by the FA as the first after he was selected to play for England schoolboys as a 15-year-old, against Northern Ireland at Wembley in March 1971, six years earlier than Laurie Cunningham.

Benjamin (known as Ben or Benjy) came to England after his parents had moved over and settled in from Nigeria. Speaking in 2020, Ben said of the time in the mid-1960s: "The racism was rife, (much) worse than it is now", he remembers reading a sign on an accommodation building which read 'room to let, no Irish, no dogs, and no blacks' in that exact order. "It was showing dogs are more important than blacks. The Irish on top, dogs in the middle and blacks on the bottom. Name-calling was a standard procedure, and no non-black saw any real issue with it. Names like 'nig-nog' were bellowed at you if you were black literally as soon as you left your house. 'Coon' was another favoured derogatory slur. We had to suffer in those days, there were only four television channels. On primetime TV we used to have Alf Garnett, Love Thy Neighbour, programmes like that. The words that were being used, were not words that should be used, but they were used. The racial abuse was too numerous to mention. In those days it was just a free-for-all, even the people supposed to be looking after you, the coaches and your team-mates, referred to you as chalky or sambo. The people who are supposed to be on your side were often the biggest perpetrators. You're trying to fight it but there's nowhere for you to go."

Ben was a prolific goal scorer, scoring an incredible 400 goals in three years at schoolboy level playing for South East London, Blackheath District and London Schoolboys. His astonishing talent in front of goal was recognised when the 'boy Pele' was called up to play for England Schoolboys. His historic debut came on 6th March 1971 and was in front of over 70,000 people against Northern Ireland at the FA's home of football, Wembley. An assortment of family members went to watch the historic game, but his mother was unable to attend as she had to work her shift at the local hospital.

Ben recalls how nervous he was: "When you walk onto that Wembley turf and the crowd are roaring, and the referee is ready to blow that whistle, and the whistle is blown, you are (just) thinking about your first touch. Now, if you make a mistake with that first touch, the next ten minutes you can kiss it goodbye. But if your first touch is okay, the crowd sits there and appreciates it, (then) you are gone, (it is) great. And of course all of the noise level from the crowd disappears. And then all you can hear is your teammate calling you, giving you instructions on what to do." Playing out of his usual striking position, Ben played on the wing and helped England to a 1-0 victory, making such an impression that he was voted 'Man of the Match'.

Although starring for England, Ben recalls travelling home along Oxford Street a few hours later when a man walked past him and called him a 'black bastard'. Ben said of the incident: "A few hours ago I was on the Wembley turf, wearing a white shirt with the Three Lions on it. I was regarded (I suppose) as an Englishman. But now I am in my street clothes, I am a black human being or a black bastard."

Photo: Ben's headline before his England debut

Ben went on to play four more times for England schoolboys, but never managed to break into the senior team at Charlton. Instead he went on to play for non-league sides Dulwich Hamlet, Hendon and Clapton. Signing for Dulwich Hamlet in 1974, Ben recalls how racist some of the crowds were. He said of the racism: “It’s the fact that a ‘black’ player is actually playing and hurting a team that they support, they would do everything humanly possible to disrupt your game. Bananas would be thrown at you, money chants every time the ball was passed to you. Or they would call you names like ‘coon’ or ‘nigger boy’”.

Ben said he would try and block out the insults and just play football. Any banana that hit him or came near him, he would eat half of it and throw it back in the direction it came from. Ben thought that a lot of the racism, even from within his own camp was due to a lack of education. He said: “I must admit the coaches even though they would use ‘chalky’ and names like that, they actually never meant it to hurt us. For some of them it’s the fear of the unknown, because they did not know what they were doing, for some of them it was a joke. During my time I could not complain to anyone, because who would I complain to?”

After he finished playing Ben went to work for Queens Park Rangers and was one of the founding members of their ‘Football in the Community’ scheme. After leaving QPR he started his own soccer school Atlantic Sports Development.

To recognise Ben’s importance in the history of English football, the FA paid tribute to him and the other black trailblazers at Wembley by either having them present or represented by family during the England versus Germany UEFA Nations League game on 26 September 2022.

JOHN CHARLES (WEST HAM)

John Charles (Charlo) was born in Canning Town in 1944, the son of a seaman from Grenada and an English mother who was on her third marriage. Charlo said of his family situation: “I was number eight of nine children, all different colours. There was Jessie, Josie, Bon, Len, Bonzo, Marge and Rita. Clive (who would also play for West Ham) came later... The four eldest were white (there were five, Michael got killed); then there was Bonzo and Margie, they were sort of tan, their dad was black but they didn't come out that way. They were olive colour. My dad was black but we came out black."

Charlo signed his first professional contract for West Ham in April 1962, and the following month on 20 May 1962 England Under-18’s beat Israel 3-1 in Tel Aviv. Charlo started and scored. He featured in the return fixture against the same opponents two days later, when England lost 2-1. A year later England won the UEFA Under-18 tournament on home soil for the second time in their history. Charlo played in a 2-0 victory in the last group game against the Soviet Union.

In 1963 aged 18, he was given his first-team debut at left-back for West Ham by manager Ron Greenwood against Blackburn Rovers in front of a crowd 18,898 people. He then went on to captain the West Ham youth team to cup glory when they beat Liverpool in the 1963 FA Youth Cup final. Former West Ham player and later manager, Harry Redknapp said of the win and the influence Charlo had by saying: “In those days winning the FA Youth tournament was massive. Charlo was a great leader for us because most of us were younger than him, so in a way we looked up to him. He read the game well and he was a tough lad. If you got tackled by John you would know about it. He liked to enjoy himself, and Bobby Moore and all of the other lads loved him. The whole team at West Ham in those days used to come from within about five miles from the football ground. We either came from Poplar, Canning Town, Barking, or Dagenham.” Another teammate from the Youth Cup winning team was forward Martin Britt who scored four goals in the second leg of the final, he said of his captain: “Charlo was tough as old boots and he was well known for his tackling and not taking any prisoners. In those days I can’t really recall playing against another black player. No one looked at Charlo as a black person, we just looked at him as John. He was one of the lads and honestly everyone loved him.”

Although he did face incidents of racism Charlo said: "I never remember any real racism, certainly not from other players at West Ham or our crowd. Maybe some players respond to it too quickly and become a target when everyone knows it winds them up. If they'd just keep playing they would stop... The idea that West Ham fans are racist is rubbish! They didn't ask if you were black or white; they asked if you were West Ham." Martin Britt did witness some of the racism though and said of the abuse “When we used to go places sometimes they would be rude to Charlo and it used to upset us more than it upset him, I remember playing at Ipswich for West Ham’s reserves and John was playing and there was this guy on the sidelines shouting terrible stuff. There was only about 7,000 or 8,000 people there but most of us could hear what he was saying. He was calling Charlo the N-word and everything under the sun. So the ball went out on the sideline and John Bond jumped over the sideline, got hold of the guy and said: “If I fucking hear you say that again, I’m going to thump you.” He got back on the pitch and the referee applauded him.”

Charlo would go on to play 118 times in the West Ham first team and was a great fixture within the club. He said there was a drinking culture during his time at West Ham in which he was a big part. The group mainly consisted of Bobby Moore, Johnny Byrne, John Cushley, Harry Redknapp, Brian Dear and himself. He said of the way of life at the time: "We were always on the piss. We went from the club to the pub. I was part of a hard-drinking crowd... Everyone liked a drink... You didn't even think about it. It was second nature."

Later in his career Charlo suffered a lot from hamstring problems and at the premature age of 26 he decided to retire from football. After he finished he went to work with his father-in-law who ran his own green-grocery business. "At West Ham, I was earning £65 a week. My first week as a barrow boy, I got £200. I started with Carol's (his wife's) dad. Once I got into that lark, I really loved it. I became my own governor."

Photo: John Charles (back row third from the right) in the West Ham side with World Cup winners, Martin Peters (top left), Geoff Hurst (front row second from right) and Bobby Moore (back row far right).

Unfortunately there was no happy ending to Charlo's story, his business eventually got into trouble: "I soon had stalls all over Kent, but then they started to open the supermarkets and we went skint... I was an alcoholic and in the end I had a breakdown. I was so bad, once, in hospital, I dreamed I was eating my sister in a sandwich!" He left hospital just before his 50th birthday and gained employment in his local supermarket where he was considered a hero. Charlo who was a heavy smoker, was diagnosed with cancer in October 2001 and he died from the illness aged 57 on 17 August 2002. His former teammate and drinking buddy, Brian Dear said at Charlo's funeral: "Football is surely indebted to him as he undoubtedly paved the way for his black brothers who now enjoy the fame, riches and adulation, which he most certainly helped make possible."

THE ENGLAND CALL UP THAT NEVER WAS

Viv Anderson is officially recognised by the Football Association as the first black player to play for the full England side, but John (Jack) Leslie (1901-1988) who was born in Canning Town, London to a Jamaican father and English mother had been initially selected for England in 1925.

Jack had signed for Plymouth Argyle in 1921 and would go on to make 384 appearances scoring 133 goals in fourteen seasons with Argyle. In October 1925, during his fourth successful season he was called up for the England squad, and although it was never officially confirmed, he was ultimately denied an England appearance because of the colour of his skin. At the time Jack was both surprised and delighted to be called up for England. He said in a rare interview with the Daily Mail about the call-up:

"Well, one day, a Tuesday as I remember, the manager, Mr Bob Jack, calls me in. He's looking over his glasses and smiling. He stands up and puts his arms on my shoulder. "Johnnie" – that's what he called me – "Johnnie… I've got great news for you. You've been picked for England."

'This really knocked me sideways. Everybody in the club knew about it. The town was full of it. All them days ago, it was quite a thing for a little club like Plymouth to have a man called up for England. I was proud — but then I was proud just to be a paid footballer."

Jack's selection as one of two travelling reserves to play against Ireland was published in the press, with the Westminster Gazette writing that it was an 'interesting feature' that a 'man of colour' was selected.

A few days after the squad was announced, news of an injury to Huddersfield left-back Sam Wadsworth would mean his withdrawal from the squad. *The Western Daily Press* reported the news as such:

Photo: Jack Leslie in action for Plymouth Argyle

'A substitute, of course, will now have to be found, and it is not unlikely that Leslie, the darkie (sic) forward of Plymouth Argyle, will fill the vacancy' Within a weeks' notice of Wadsworth's withdrawal from the England squad *The Athletic News* reported on the England squad, but Jack's name had mysteriously disappeared. The reserves chosen to travel were now named as Nuttall and Earle and there was no mention of Jack in the squad at all. Jack was neither injured nor suspended and no explanation was given as to why he wasn't in the squad. England went on to play out a 0-0 draw in a Home Championship game in front of 30,000 people on 24 October 1925 at Windsor Park Belfast.

The same day Jack starred for Plymouth in a Third Division South fixture, scoring twice in a home 7-2 victory over Bournemouth in front of 10,693 fans. Although most of the press avoided reporting Jack's omission, it still caused a controversy. *The Daily Herald* tried to investigate but the Football Association (FA) denied they'd ever picked Jack while the Press Association were resolute that they had. The reporter from the Herald suggestively commented that the football authorities wanted to draw a veil over the whole episode by saying:

'My readers may be expecting from me a comment upon Argyle Club's announcement that Jack Leslie was not chosen as a reserve forward for England. Unfortunately, my pen is under a ban in this matter, but I may say that a mistake was made in London and transmitted to me. Anyway, Leslie was at that time playing quite well enough to be chosen.'

Jack was never given any official explanation about his eventual omission from the squad but many years later said of the incident:

"Then all of a sudden everyone stopped talking about it. Sort of went dead quiet. Didn't look me in the eye. I didn't ask outright. I could see by their faces it was awkward. But I did hear, roundabout like that the FA had come to have another look at me. Not at me football but at me face. They asked, and found they'd made a ricket. Found out about me daddy, and that was it. There was a bit of an uproar in the papers. Folks in the town were very upset. No one ever told me official-like, but that had to be the reason, me mum was English but me daddy was black as the Ace of Spades. There wasn't any other reason for taking my cap away".

As it unfolded, Jack never won an England cap. *The Daily Mail* ran an article towards the end of Jack's illustrious career in 1933 in which it commented that the 'coloured genius, had he been white he would have been a certain England international.' It would be another 53 years before a black player would be selected for the full England squad. Viv Anderson the Nottingham Forest right-back made history when he was picked for as the first black player to win a full England cap when he played in a friendly game against Czechoslovakia in 1978.

It should be noted that Leeds United right back Paul Reaney was the first non-white player to play for the full England team when as a player of mixed race he was selected to play against Bulgaria on 11 December 1968. Jack who retired from professional football in 1935 was remembered by the legendary West Ham United boss Ron Greenwood in the 1960s who offered him a job in the boot room at Upton Park.

Jack accepted and worked with some of the West Ham legends like World Cup winners, Bobby Moore, Geoff Hurst and Martin Peters. Jack was also able to pass on his experiences and prejudices he faced in football to legendary forward Clyde Best. Best himself was one of the first black players in the First Division and was regularly targeted with racist chanting from the terraces. Jack worked at West Ham until he retired aged 80. As fate would have it, Ron Greenwood who offered the West Ham job to Jack, became the England manager in 1977 and be the first person to pick a black player for the national squad. The pioneering Jack Leslie was remembered when the boardroom at the newly developed Home Park stadium in Plymouth was named after him.

In November 2020 a blue plaque was unveiled outside his former home in Canning Town.

On the same day a 12-foot bronze statue of Jack was unveiled at Home Park. In 2023, he was inducted into the National Football Museum's Hall of Fame with the FA stating: “it was to recognise his unique contribution and set of circumstances – and to right the historical wrong."

Jack was posthumously awarded an England cap 97 years after he was called up. Prior to England's Euro 2024 qualifier against Ukraine at Wembley on 26 March 2023, Jack's family were presented with his long overdue cap.

The last word from Jack on the shameful episode came before his death when he said in an interview:

“They must have forgot I was a coloured boy.”

Photo: Bronze Statue of Jack Leslie outside Home Park, Plymouth.

ALBERT SETTLES IN

Albert was buoyed after his successful debut against Swansea, but the burden from apartheid was still weighing heavily upon him. Notwithstanding his new found freedom, he was still finding it difficult to accept that he was now allowed to mix with people regardless of their nationalities and colour, and was able to go places he wouldn't be allowed to in South Africa.

In the following week's training after his successful debut, Revie informed Albert that both he and Gerry Francis would be playing on the Saturday away at Stoke City. Albert was delighted with the vote of confidence from Revie and also that he would be able to play in the same team as his good friend Gerry who was selected to play on the opposite wing. Albert and Gerry knew the occasion would be special and unique. Both players were excited at the prospect of two black South African footballers playing in the same team in a competitive league fixture for the first time. Albert was selected on the left wing and Gerry on the right wing.

Their hope was that their selection would send out a positive message to countless black children across the world giving them hope about their own aspirations and possibilities.

Arriving for the game at Stoke with optimism, Albert said he was treated really badly. On his way into the ground he said he was verbally accosted with insults such as: 'What are you doing here? Are you here to clean shoes or what?' and 'Look at what we have here boys, a little negro, where's your spear Zulu man?' Scared and confused, he quickly got himself into the ground, but even inside the stadium Albert said he received a barrage of abuse throughout the day.

A dull goalless draw was played out on a wet and muddy pitch, and although there was very little fuss about it at the time, both Albert and Gerry were proud that they had made history in being the first two black footballers to play together in the same team in an English football league fixture.

Dealing with racism in football was at the time without precedent, and the players didn't know who to turn to for help. In the 1960s there were no sports psychologists and mental health wasn't something that was openly discussed. A common way to cope with pressures at the time was through alcohol which created a 'drinking culture'. With time on their hands after training and with little outside support or education, many players succumbed to alcohol addiction, most notably George Best, Jimmy Greaves and unfortunately in time Albert.

Being in the spotlight constantly had its drawbacks. On one occasion after Albert had been called a 'black bastard' by an opponent he complained to Don Revie. Revie's advice was to simply reply to the insult by calling the offender a 'white bastard' in return, he said in that way they would be then equal. Albert wasn't satisfied with the response but he said whenever he approached Revie about the abuse he was receiving he was just told that he had to deal with it, and to ingratiate himself with people. Although he said the advice he was receiving was not very helpful he didn't think Revie was being malicious, but he did find it disrespectful.

Billy Bremner who was a great support to Albert would advise him to answer the abuse by playing even better, and although Albert would try and take the advice, for somebody of such a nervous disposition and full of self-doubt, this simplistic approach would ultimately be of little help to him. But regardless he had begun to make his mark on the field and finished the 1960-61 season by playing in all of Leeds final five games in which they only lost one, the final game at Charlton:

8/4/61 – Swansea Town home drew 2-2 (Charlton 2) att 11,862,
15/4/61 - Stoke City away drew 0-0 att 7,130,
22/4/61 - Lincoln City home won 7-0 (McCole 2 - 1 pen, Bell, Peyton, McConnell, Bremner Drysdale og) att 8,432,
25/4/61 – Scunthorpe United home drew 2-2 (McCole 2) att 6,975,
29/4/61 – Charlton Athletic away lost 2-0 att 9,081.

The Stoke game was to be the only time Albert and Gerry would play together at Leeds as Gerry wasn't in Revie's future plans and he was sold to York City in October 1961. The historical game in which two black South Africans had played together in an English league game had the press dubbing Albert and Gerry as the 'Johannesburg Twins'.

From the beginning Don Revie had a big job on his hands with Leeds struggling in the second division. Attendances at Elland Road had been dwindling, and they recorded what is still their lowest post-war crowd when only 6,975 people turned out for the last home game of the season against Scunthorpe United. This was even after they had beaten Lincoln 7-0 at home three days previous. It was the lowest home attendance since

1934, and gave Revie and Chairman Harry Reynolds plenty to think about over the summer. Although at this point not large in number, Albert had become a home crowd favourite in a short time, with regular chants of 'Albert, Albert' ringing around the ground. This was tempered though with the abuse he was receiving from away fans at Elland Road and from supporters at away grounds. In his excellent book *'100 years of Leeds United'*, Daniel Chapman said of the time 'Apart from Grenville Hair, an institution for ten seasons at full-back, only Albert Johanneson offered any hope on the pitch. Johanneson made the wing lively; he was fast, direct, had tricks defenders hadn't seen and scored more goals than many centre-forwards. But the rest of the team was as stale as Johanneson was fresh'. Albert's stock was continuing to rise, but even with his flair, Don Revie knew the size of the task ahead with a struggling second division team. But he was determined to reconstruct the club from the ground up, developing the club from within. Although he was always on the look out to bring new players into Leeds, he knew that long term he had to bring players through the youth system to be able to compete with the more established clubs.

Photo: Leeds United juniors 1963-64 **Back Row:** Terry Hibbitt, Jimmy Lumsden, Bobby Sibbald, David Harvey, John Price, Mick Bates, Dennis Hawkins. **Front Row:** Graham Smith, Eddie Gray, Jimmy Greenhoff, Barrie Wright, Peter Lorimer, Nigel Davey, Derek Ryder, Rod Belfitt.

ALBERT'S FIRST FULL SEASON 1961-62

With Leeds narrowly avoiding relegation to the third division, Don Revie looked to shake up the Leeds squad. He brought in the experienced Tommy Younger (Toronto City), Billy McAdams (Bolton Wanderers), Ian Lawson (Burnley), Cliff Mason (Sheffield United).

Revie is said to have changed the Leeds kit from their blue and gold strip to an all-white strip to transform the underachieving club into the Real Madrid of Yorkshire starting by copying the Spanish giant's kit. But there is another version of the white kit story in that the previous manager, Jack Taylor had first deployed the use of the all-white kit the previous season when they used the change kit of all-white in September 1960. At first the white kit was worn without a badge but in 1964 a badge with an Owl was added which represented the coat of arms of Leeds.

Albert started to shine in the white kit, and he got off to a good start in the 1961-62 season playing in the first seven matches. Leeds started well with two victories, but a winless run of five games set them back:

19/8/61 - Charlton at home 1-0 (Bremner) att 12,916,

22/8/61 - Brighton and Hove Albion away 3-1 (Peyton, Bremner, Mayers) att 22,744,

26/8/61 - Liverpool away lost 5-0 att 42,450,

30/8/61 - Brighton home drew 1-1(Bremner) att 12,642,

2/9/61 - Rotherham home lost 3-1(McCole) att 12,610,

6/9/61 - Norwich City away lost 2-0 att 26,860,

9/9/61 - Sunderland away lost 2-1(McCole) att 30,737.

After only seven games Leeds were sitting precariously in 19th place in the table, and after flirting with relegation the previous season, Revie felt forced into making changes.

Billy Bremner recalled: “Albert had no confidence. He could play, he was bloody quick, and Bobby Collins could sometimes get him up, get him going. But it was as if Albert couldn't believe it was happening to him, as if he thought a black man wasn't entitled to be famous.”

After a run of three straight defeats, Albert was dropped after Sunderland had given Leeds a torrid time at Roker Park, in which Albert had been particularly targeted and had picked up a couple of knocks in front of a crowd of over thirty thousand. Albert said the passionate but ill-educated crowd were continually chanting Zulu warrior sounds at him throughout the game.

He was disappointed at being dropped from the side, thinking he was being made the scapegoat for Leeds poor performances. He tried again to speak to Don Revie about the abuse he was receiving but he said Revie just asked him to go away and reflect on what he wanted and how he planned to make progress.

Having been dropped, Albert was feeling alone and saddened and was considering a returning to South Africa. His mood wasn’t helped when his good friend, Gerry Francis was transferred to York City. Albert felt Gerry’s transfer affected him more than it did Gerry and with his fragile ego he started to think that he would be next out of the door.

In Albert’s place came former England youth international, John Hawksby who had a run of 22 games from 13 September 1961 through to

9 April 1962. Albert played in only one game in that period replacing Billy McAdams in a League Cup 4th round replay tie at home to Rotherham.

Albert scored his first ever Leeds goal from the penalty spot in the Rotherham game of which he said: "One highlight of the season was scoring my first-ever goal for the club. It was a penalty kick in a League Cup game against Rotherham United. We lost 2-1, and scoring from the penalty spot isn't always seen as spectacular or skill-orientated goal, but it was special for me because it was my first. It was met with little in the way of celebration but remains a personal milestone of my career."

15/1/62 - Rotherham League Cup Round 4 Replay home lost 2-1 (Johanesson pen) att 6,385.

Albert missed the following 1-0 win at home to Sunderland, but made a return to the first team the following week on 27 January 1962 when he replaced the injured John Hawksby in a 1-0 home defeat against Newcastle United.

27/1/62 - Newcastle United lost 1-0 att 17,120

Albert wouldn't play in the first team again until 14 April 1962 when he again regained his place at the expense of Hawksby away at Walsall. With Leeds sitting in 20th place in Division 2, just one place above a relegation spot, Albert scored a vital goal in front of a crowd of 9,005 in a 1-1 draw. Although still in jeopardy of relegation Revie made what turned out to be the inspirational signing of thirty-one-year-old Bobby Collins from Everton for £25,000 in March 1962. The signing of Collins was a masterstroke. He had been deemed as past his best after four years at

Everton, but he was the catalyst in Revie's revolution after first staving off relegation in the final months of the season. Standing at barely 5ft 4in, weighing around 10 stone and wearing size four boots, Collins was the perfect foil for Albert's skill and pace. His aggression and pinpoint passing would give Albert the ammunition he needed for his fast and creative style.

Collins part in Leeds revival cannot be overestimated, with Don Revie saying of him: "He's the perfect example of what we in the game call a professional's professional. Bobby's aim was always to do things simply and quickly in the field, he never tried to be too clever on the ball for the sake of his own glory. I have never come across anyone with such a fierce will-to-win and dedication to the game… Bobby regarded it as a personal insult to be beaten - we had numerous kicking bouts when I played against him for Manchester City! As manager of Leeds, I had been searching for some time for a midfield general with the character and skill really to motivate the team, and Bobby fitted the bill perfectly." Collins was an inspiration at Leeds even going on to win the Footballer of the Year award in 1965 aged thirty-four. Revie would later say about Collins: "The best signing I ever made. Leeds can never thank him enough for the transformation he brought to the club."

Collins said of Albert on his arrival at Leeds: "When I first came to Leeds the boys mentioned a young coloured lad, I started watching him, he was really… he was gonna be a player! He was a lovely player to play with honestly. It was just one of those things, you can meet a guy in your life, and you can fire the ball and you know he's going to run for it. He didn't hesitate, it was terrific."

With Bobby Collins pulling the strings in midfield, he created a great understanding with Albert. Collins later said of the partnership: "Albert could fly and I could put the ball on the spot for him. When he was in his stride there weren't many who could catch him."

The 1-1 draw with Walsall on 14 April 1962 was of particular note in Albert's career when he scored his first league goal, the first of forty-eight league goals he would score throughout his Leeds career.

14/4/62 Walsall away drew 1-1 (Johanneson) att 9,005.

After the draw with Walsall, Phil Brown noted in the *Yorkshire Evening Post*: "On the brighter side of things there is the great advance of 21-year-old Albert Johanneson. Albert is the first to admit he has something to learn yet, but he is learning, and he has plenty of natural gifts to help him. When did you last see a winger stop in full stride so shatteringly?"

With only four games of the season left Leeds had moved up one place to 19th but were still in danger of relegation to the Third Division.

Albert retained his place in the side for the last four games (played in eight days, including 2 on consecutive days) and he played a pivotal role in Leeds unbeaten end to the season. It included an impressive 3-0 away win at Newcastle on the last day of the season in which Albert scored the first goal. The report for the game stated: "Albert Johanneson was a key figure in a performance of collective discipline. Johanneson's first half goal on 37 minutes, a header from Johanneson's cross by McAdams after 65 minutes and an own goal by Newcastle right-back Bobby Keith ten minutes later, gave Revie deliverance."

Leeds finished the 1961-62 season in 19th place just 3 points above relegation. The final four games were:

20/4/62 - Bury away drew 1-1 (Charlton) att 11,313,
21/4/62 - Derby County home drew 0-0 att 11,922,
24/4/62 - Bury home drew 0-0 21,482,
28/4/62 - Newcastle United away won 3-0 (Johanneson, McAdams, Keith o.g) att 21,708.

Albert was creating headlines and was in great demand. Leeds had finished the 1961-62 in good form going unbeaten in their last 9 games (won 3 drew 6). Revie had started to put a strong team together while also identifying where he needed to strengthen. He knew that a winning team would bring back the crowds to Elland Road, but with Leeds struggling they recorded their two lowest average attendances since the 1920s (1960-61 – 13,443 and 1961-62 – 13,607). Revie also knew that higher attendances would generate a higher income which could then be used to strengthen his squad. Albert having seen off the challenge of the highly rated John Hawksby who would only play in seven further games for Leeds before he was eventually sold to Lincoln City in August 1964.

Overall, Albert's first full season in professional football had gone well. He had ingratiated himself with his fellow Leeds players and was becoming a favourite with the Elland Road faithful. He had played in thirteen league games and had scored twice. He had also scored his first goal in professional football with a penalty which he scored in his only cup appearance of the season against Rotherham United in the League Cup.

Having finished the season well and achieving his ambition of a professional contract in England, Albert was given dispensation by Revie to take a summer break back home in South Africa. His family were thrilled to have him home and it seemed that everyone in Germiston was delighted with his success in England. While back home, Albert didn't divulge any of the abuse he had received while in England as he didn't want to spoil the image of the life that his fellow South African's imagined that he was having. Albert wanted his success to be uplifting and inspirational to his fellow black South Africans.

Photo: Leeds United 1962

Back Row: Grenville Hair, Paul Reaney, Gary Sprake, Jack Charlton, Willie Bell, Norman Hunter.

Front Row: Tommy Henderson, Albert Johanneson, Jim Storrie, Bobby Collins, Billy Bremner.

1962-63 ALBERT'S A NEW BEGINNING

On his arrival back in England, Albert set about his pre-season training with his usual vigour and was happy to be back in Leeds.

Don Revie had brought back the Welsh legend John Charles to Leeds in a club record £53,000 deal after five years with Juventus in Italy (where he scored 108 goals in 155 appearances).

Albert said of John Charles: "He took an instant liking to me and tended to look after me. He told me to watch my back and trust no one."

Revie also drafted in four teenagers from the youth team that they were hoping to develop - goalkeeper Gary Sprake, right-back Paul Reaney, left-half Norman Hunter and centre-forward Rodney Johnson.

Albert started the season well playing in a 1-0 away win at Stoke with the *Yorkshire Post* reporting: "Johanneson, a fast and dextrous ball player... looked and often played like some rising star from Brazil. Before long Asprey was casting quick suspicious glances over his shoulder - even when the ball was elsewhere - as though Johanneson were some angry wasp, not to be trusted."

Albert continued his great start to the season by scoring in the next game, a 4-3 defeat at home to Rotherham. His stock was rising immensely and was highlighted with the report on the defeat saying: "the brightest features were the hard working displays of Collins and Johanneson".

Albert set up the winner for Billy Bremner in the next game in a 1-0 win against Sunderland, and the next three games produced a draw at Huddersfield 1-1, a loss at home to Bury 2-1 and a 2-0 away win at Swansea.

Albert grabbed the headlines in the next game when he starred and scored twice in a big 2-0 win over promotion favourites Chelsea who had been relegated the previous season. The first goal was described as a 'beauty' with the *Evening Post* reporting it as follows:

"Charles brought the ball up from halfway, Peyton swept in to join him going left and passed out to the left winger (Albert). He dodged round three desperate tacklers like an eel and coming up to his near post popped the ball gently past Bonetti."

The *Yorkshire Post* was also full of praise for Albert saying: "The man who brought the crowd to their feet was Johanneson, scorer of both goals, and the first United player I have seen applauded by his teammates as he trotted to the dressing room."

Although they were showing promise the new Leeds side were inconsistent in their first fifteen games, of which Albert played in 12 of them. He missed the defeat at Rotherham three days after beating Sunderland when he said he came in for some rough treatment and was particularly targeted, in his words he was "kicked off the field."

He said as early as the second minute he was punched in the back of the head by a Sunderland player and called 'darkie'. Albert also alleged that the Sunderland manager, Alan Brown approached him after the game and offered to 'make him a better player than he had ever been' and that he didn't think that he would have been able to stand up to the rough treatment they had targeted towards him, but complemented him on being able to do so. Albert said he was flattered by the approach but he had started to settle and his love of Leeds and the football club had become too strong to the point that he didn't to want to leave.

Albert's first twelve appearances of 1962-63:

18/8/62 - Stoke City away won 1-0 (Storrie) att 27,118,
22/8/62 - Rotherham United home lost 4-3 (Storrie Charles, Johanesson) att 14,119,
25/8/62 - Sunderland home won 1-0 (Bremner) att 17,753,
1/9/62 - Huddersfield Town away drew 1-1 (Charles) att 34,946,
5/9/62 - Bury home lost 2-1 (Bremner) att 28,313,
8/9/62 - Swansea Town away won 2-0 (Johnson, Bremner) att 17,696
15/9/62 - Chelsea home win 2-0 (Johanesson 2) att 27,520
18/9/62 - Bury away lost 3-1 (Storrie) att 18,876,
22/9/62 - Luton Town away drew 2-2 (Storrie, Collins) att 8,958,
29/9/62 - Southampton home drew 1-1(Storrie) att 25,408
6/10/62 - Middlesbrough home lost 3-2 (Hunter, Bremner) att 28,222
13/10/62 - Derby County away drew 0-0 att 14,246.

Albert would go on to play in every league game of 1961-62 apart from the 2-1 away defeat at Rotherham on 28 August which he missed through injury. He played in forty-one league games in total.

John Charles had made a good start on his return to Elland Road, scoring 3 goals in his first 5 games. But his return turned out to be a lot less successful than his original period when he had scored 157 goals in 297 appearances. So, after only 11 appearances and 3 goals, in October 1962 when an offer came in from Roma in Italy (where Charles was still revered), Leeds happily sold him for £70,000.

Leeds hierarchy were aware that they were losing a great player and a big attraction, but they were happy to come out of the deal with a tidy profit.

On the field, Leeds were showing a lot of inconsistency to this point and were hovering in mid-table, but Charles' departure was a surprising catalyst for an improvement in results. Leeds would go on to lose only 5 of their next 25 league fixtures.

Albert would make a great impression in the 1962-63 season and cemented his place in an emerging and confident Leeds side. By 4 May 1963 a much improved Leeds were in fourth place pushing for one of the two promotion places. They were only 3 points behind leaders Stoke and 2 points behind second place Chelsea with four games to go. In the 25 games in which Leeds lost 5 games, Albert played in them all scoring an impressive 9 goals (5 in the first 7 after John Charles left):

20/10/62 - Newcastle United home won 1-0 (Johanneson) att 23,286,

27/10/62 - Walsall away drew 1-1 (Johanneson) att 7,353,

3/11/62 - Norwich City home won 3-0 (Johanneson, Bell, Storrie) att 15,919,

10/11/62 - Grimsby Town away drew 1-1 (Storrie) 9,183

17/11/62 - Plymouth Argyle home won 6-1 (Johanneson, Storrie 3, Collins, Bremner) att 15,301,

24/11/62 - Preston North End away lost 4-1 (Bell) 13,145,

1/12/62 - Portsmouth home drew 3-3 (Johanneson, Collins, Storrie) att 15,519

8/12/62 - Cardiff City away drew 0-0 att 11,334

15/12/62 - Stoke City home won 3-1 (Weston 3) att 19,331,

22/12/62 - Sunderland away lost 2-1 (Bremner) att 40,252.

Albert was still acclimatising himself to the weather in England and struggling with the cold. It didn't help with the winter of 1962-63 being a particularly harsh one with one of the coldest winters on record.

Albert recalled in an interview in Buchan's *Football Monthly* in 1962: "All the time I was trying to get used to heavy pitches, matches in sludge and rain."

Temperatures plummeted for weeks on end, causing rivers, lakes and even the sea to freeze over. The weather hadn't stopped Albert putting in a string of great performances, and even though he was still receiving abuse from unruly supporters both at Elland Road and at away games, he carried himself with great style and composure.

The first few weeks of December 1962 had been changeable and stormy, but fixtures were still able to go ahead. This changed when snow hit England on Boxing Day, it would see fixtures cancelled throughout the whole of January and February, with the league programme not commencing again until March 1963.

Leeds first game back upon the snow clearing was on March 2. The break appeared to have done them good as a run of 4 wins and a draw would build their confidence further. It was a hectic finish to the season with fixtures having to be fitted in after all the postponed games.

Leeds would have to play on average every 3 days for their final 22 matches. Fixture pile-ups like this often occurred for successful sides throughout the 1960s and 1970s. This aligned with the fact that substitutes still weren't allowed meant that players would often have to play on with injuries resulting in a lot of careers being shortened through the physical demand.

Leeds results on resumption of fixtures:

2/3/63 - Derby County home won 3-1 (Weston, Storrie, Charlton pen) att 22,912,

6/3/63 - Stoke City FA Cup round 3 home won 3-1 (Collins, Reaney, Hair) att 36,873 (largest home crowd of the season),

9/3/63 - Newcastle United away drew 1-1 (Storrie) att 29,570,

13/3/63 - Walsall away won 3-0 (Johanneson, Storrie 2) att 17,077

16/3/63 - Middlesbrough FA Cup round 4 away won 2-0 (Johanneson, Storrie) att 39,672,

19/3/63 - Nottingham Forest FA Cup round 5 away lost 3-0 att 36,392,

23/3/63 - Norwich City away lost 3-2 (Johanneson, Collins) att 26,154,

30/3/63 - Grimsby Town home won 3-0 Collins 2, Bremner) att 13,938,

3/4/63 - Scunthorpe United home won 1-0 (Bremner) att 15,783,

6/4/63 - Plymouth Argyle away lost 3-1 (Storrie) att 8,992.

The intense run of fixtures continued through April into May with Leeds playing a unique set of fixtures when they played 3 games in 4 days (Saturday, Monday and Tuesday) winning all 3 and scoring 10 goals in the process. The games included back-to-back home and away fixtures against Charlton Athletic in which Albert made his fiftieth league appearance on 15 April. The wins took them into 8th place in the table:

13/4/63 - Preston North End home won 4-1 (Bremner 2, Storrie, Collins) att 16,016,

15/4/63 - Charlton Athletic away won 2-1 (Charlton, Hunter) att 13,538,

16/4/63 - Charlton Athletic home won 4-1 (Johanneson, Weston, Henderson, Storrie) att 24,646,

20/4/63, - Portsmouth away lost 3-0 att 7,773,

23/4/63 - Scunthorpe United away won 2-0 (Lawson 2) att 7,794,

27/4/63 - Cardiff City Home won 3-0 (Storrie 3) att 19,752,

30/4/63 - Chelsea away drew 2-2 (Lawson 2) att 24,387,

4/5/63 - Luton Town home won 3-0 (Storrie 2, Weston) att 23,781.

After such a rigorous run of fixtures, and with only four games left to play, Leeds had put themselves in with a strong chance of promotion. Sitting in fourth place they had beaten Luton on the Saturday but faced a tough trip away to Middlesbrough two days later on the Monday. Fatigue appeared to be taking its toll and although Albert scored they were beaten 2-1. Two further defeats followed and their promotion push came to a shuddering halt. A thumping 5-0 final win in the last game of the season against Swansea Town (later Swansea City in 1969), in which Albert scored again, gave Leeds an upbeat finish to what was seen as a positive season and a stepping stone to the greater times ahead.

Leeds finished fifth with attendances on the increase (20,213 average as opposed to the previous year of 13,607). There was much optimism at Elland Road for the new season to come for both Leeds and Albert.

Last four games of 1962-63:

6/5/63 - Middlesbrough away lost 2-1 (Johanneson) att 17,365,

11/5/63 - Huddersfield home lost 1-0 att 28,501,

15/5/63 - Southampton away lost 3-1 (Weston) att 11,619,

18/5/63 - Swansea Town home won 5-0 (Johanneson, Lawson, Collins, Storrie 2) att 11,314.

Albert had well and truly established himself in the team, appearing in a total of 44 games (41 league games and 3 cup games), while finishing the clubs second highest goalscorer for the season with 11 goals (Jim Storrie was top scorer with 25 league goals in 38 appearances, Billy Bremner was third with 10 league goals).

He had played in front of crowds totalling over eight hundred thousand (834,229), and although he was still facing idiotic racist chants Albert had adhered himself to the Leeds public. He had enjoyed a wonderful season, with *The Times* describing him as: "the colourful, popular, Johanneson from Johannesburg, whose gazelle-like speed down the wing draws the crowds down the terraces, an exciting player in the mould of some dusky Brazilian."

1963 was a vintage year for Albert, not only had he established himself in the Leeds United team and ingratiated himself with the Leeds faithful, but looking back Albert said that his favourite ever year was 1962. He had gained a place in the Leeds side and he had met the love of his life the beautiful, Norma Elaine Comrie. Norma was originally from Jamaica and worked as a dispenser (chemist) at the Leeds General Infirmary (LGI) in Leeds. Albert rarely discussed his family life as he considered it too personal, but he did say that he fell madly in love with Norma and she made him very happy, with the relationship containing much love and some pain. Norma was a couple of years younger than Albert but he knew as soon as they met that she was the one and only woman for him. During the big freeze of 1963 on a bitterly cold Wednesday, Albert and Norma tied the knot at Blenheim Chapel in Leeds on 27 February, before going on to hold their wedding reception in the Griffin hotel in Leeds city centre. Don Revie and most of his other football colleagues from Leeds United attended, with Grenville Hair being a big support to the very nervous groom. Albert said of the event that it was probably the first-ever black wedding that had more white people as guests than black! In a further show of how shy Albert was, when it came to his speech, Norma's mother had to get up and do his speech for him he was that nervous! With things going well at Leeds, after the wedding Albert said he felt 'more complete'. He had a beautiful wife and he had moved out of Mrs Wineley's lodgings in Beeston and settled into a nice family home in Moortown, a more affluent area of Leeds. Albert and Norma's year was topped off in the best possible way with the birth of their first child, a daughter, Yvonne, who Albert doted on calling her Vonnie.

Photo: Albert and Norma on their Wedding Day.

At the time, Norma had never understand why Albert didn't want her to attend any of the Leeds games, but when Yvonne was interviewed in America by CNN (Cable News Network) in 2015, fifty years after Albert's historic FA Cup Final appearance, she explained:

"My mother said that she always found it odd that he never wanted her to come and see him play. Now she has a better understanding of why that could have been. It now appears obvious that he wanted to protect her from hearing the racial slurs being hurled at him and similarly safeguard her from being the brunt of such ignorance. From what people have told us, we understand that there were some people who were incapable of separating the colour of his skin from how well he could play the game of football."

Yvonne continued: "They, therefore, considered him to be inferior no matter what, and consequently fair game for their abuse and disdain. Much of the racism we learned of him having had experienced apparently came from the verbal abuse from fans and some of the players on other teams. He may have experienced other forms of racism, but he wasn't one to talk openly about what he went through with us. I mean, we were children after all. I think the prejudice he experienced was something he didn't want us to know about since it wasn't directly touching our lives."

She continued, "Now that I know what I know, I think it took quite a bit of courage for him to shield his family from seeing that uglier side of the world too soon."

Albert loved being a family man, and having just turned 23 in March he was as fit and as fast as he had ever been. With a beautiful wife and daughter by his side, and Leeds under Don Revie being on the cusp of greatness, Albert was going into 1963-64 in great spirit. The Leeds team (pictured below) would form the nucleus of the side for the very successful following ten years.

Photo: Leeds United 1963

Back Row: Billy Bremner, Paul Reaney, Gary Sprake, Jack Charlton, Norman Hunter, Willie Bell.

Front Row: Johnny Giles, Don Weston, Alan Peacock, Bobby Collins, Albert Johanneson.

1963-64 ONWARDS AND UPWARDS

Albert made a blistering start to the 1963-64 season, continuing his great form from the previous season by scoring in three of the first four games. Leeds form matched Albert's and they only lost once in the first twenty-one games, and only twice in 27 games (both times to Manchester City, one league game and one League cup). Albert scored in the second game of the season in an impressive 3-0 win against Bury for their second home win in their first two starts.

The good start to the season created a buzz around Leeds and attendances were on the rise with 26,041 attending the Bury game at the end of August, and as the season progressed attendances were regularly hitting above thirty thousand. Albert was playing a major part in Leeds resurgence and played continually in the first 21 games of the season scoring an impressive nine goals:

28/8/63 - Rotherham United home won 1-0 (Weston) att 22,517,

31/8/63 - Bury home won 3-0 (Johanneson, Collins Storrie) att 26,041,

3/9/63 - Rotherham United away drew 2-2 (Johanneson, Charlton) att 14,178,

7/9/63 - Manchester City away lost 3-2 (Johanneson, Lawson) att 29,186,

11/9/63 - Portsmouth home won 3-1 (Storrie, Weston, Bremner) att 24,926,

14/9/63 - Swindon Town home drew 0-0 att 33,301,

25/9/63 - Mansfield Town home League Cup round 2 won 5-1 (Johanneson 2, Lawson 2, Bell) att 9,843,

28/9/63 - Norwich City home won 4-2 (Johanneson, Collins pen, Weston 2) att 22,804.

With an injury to Jim Storrie, author Daniel Chapman said of the time: "The team turned to left-winger Johanneson for goals. Johanneson was brilliant, withstanding the kicks that came for his skin colour as much as his skill."

A 4-2 win against Norwich, moved an impressive Leeds from fifth to second in the table with Albert in scintillating form. He was becoming a big favourite with the Leeds faithful who would sing: 'He's better than Eusébio,' in regards to the great Portuguese player Eusébio da Silva Ferreira (The Black Panther) who scored 733 goal in 745 matches, and was the runner-up of the the Ballon d'Or in 1962 and won it in 1965. Looking back on Alberts's career and his contribution to football, Eusébio said: "Generations of black footballers should look to Albert Johanneson and thank him for what he achieved."

Leeds would not drop out of the top three in Division 2 for the rest of the season. Four more consecutive wins would take them to the top of the table two weeks before Christmas, with Revie and Chairman Harry Reynold's approach of creating a family club from the top player through to every member of staff within the club, beginning to reap its rewards:

1/10/63 - Northampton Town away won 3-0 (Lawson, Weston, Collins) att 15,079,

5/10/63 - Scunthorpe away won 1-0 (Lawson) att 10,793,

9/10/63 - Middlesbrough home won 2-0 (Hunter, Collins) att 36,919,

12/10/63 - Huddersfield Town away won 2-0 (Giles, Weston) att 31,220.

Revie was building a formidable side in which Albert was a big feature. Revie's next masterstroke came when he signed Irishman Johnny Giles from Manchester United in 1963 for £33,000. Revie would eventually pair Giles with Billy Bremner in midfield in what would become one of the most imposing partnerships in European football.

Leeds continued with their impressive form. They continued their unbeaten run for the next seven games with Albert playing in all seven and scoring some crucial goals:

19/10/63 - Derby County home drew 2-2 (Charlton, Weston) att 29,864,
22/10/63 - Swansea Town home League Cup Round 3 won 2-0 (Lawson, Storrie) att 10,748,
26/10/63 - Southampton away won 4-1 (Johanneson, Giles, Lawson 2) att 18,036,
2/11/63 - Charlton Athletic home drew 1-1 (Charlton) att 32,344.

After the draw at Charlton the *Times* reported on Albert's display: "He showed all the flair and loose-limbed speed for the game. High of action, he moved with supple grace, his feet scarcely touching the ground as if it were hot coal."

9/11/63 - Grimsby Town away won 2-0 (Lawson, Weston) att 12,194,
16/11/63 - Preston North End home drew 1-1 (Johanneson) att 33,841,
23/11/63 - Leyton Orient away won 2-0 (Johanneson, Collins) att 12,072.

Leeds received only their second defeat of the season (3-1) when Albert was rested for a League Cup match away at Manchester City on 27 October 1963. After the defeat to City they went on a five game unbeaten run with

Albert scoring two vital goals in the first two games on his return to the side:

30/11/63 - Swansea Town home won 2-1 (Johanneson, Bell) att 21,870,

7/12/63 - Plymouth Argyle away won 1-0 (Johanneson) att 9,918.

The *Evening Post* reported on the Plymouth game: "Johanneson received a special encouraging cheer whenever United tried to get him into action ... If he showed the same front of goal steadiness more often, his already considerable fan club at Elland Road would rapidly grow... Johanneson has the speed and ability to perplex the majority of opposing full-backs, and he has been in Second Division football long enough for United to hope that the time is not far off when he will add the front-of-goal temperament which is all he needs to become as deadly a menace as Southampton's international right wingman Terry Paine... From the throw in United worked the ball out to Johanneson, who moved infield with a splendid dribble. His way was barred by three Argyle defenders, but he foxed the lot of them with a clever change of direction before driving a beautiful right foot shot just inside McLaren's right hand post with the goalkeeper groping helplessly. It was a splendid goal, and no wonder the United supporters began to chant 'Albert! Albert!'."

14/12/63 - Northampton Town home drew 0-0 21,108,

21/12/63 - Bury away won 2-1 (Lawson, Weston) att 7,453,

26/12/63 - Sunderland home drew 1-1 (Lawson) att 41,167.

Leeds faced their main fellow promotion hopefuls Sunderland twice in two days over the 1963 Christmas period, firstly in front of their highest crowd of the season at Elland Road when 41,167 attended on 26 December to see a closely fought 1-1 draw, it was another game against their arch rivals from Roker Park in which Albert would receive targeted rough treatment from the Sunderland players.

Two days later on 28 December in Sunderland a crowd of 55,046 saw Leeds lose for only the second time in the league, going down 2-0. Don Revie had decided to drop Albert for the away fixture at Sunderland, saying that he thought Albert was 'too weak' to play against a bullying team like Sunderland. It was said to the press that Albert was injured but although he had taken a knock he said he was fit to play.

In a possible sign of what was to come in later years, Albert said he was angry and upset by Revie's decision to drop him, and although he rarely drank alcohol he said he went out and drowned his sorrows.

Feeling rough for several days after the session, he vowed never to drink again.

Revie was right in the assessment of what the game would amount to. Ken Jones report on the game in the *Daily Mirror* read:

"The brutal promotion battle of Roker Park was a disgrace to soccer."

Charles Summerbell also in the *Daily Mirror* stated:

"It was the most violent brawl I have ever witnessed."

And Eric Sangster in the *Yorkshire Evening Post* opined:

"I hope there are no more games like that at Roker Park on Saturday, it was full of spite and malice and overstepped the bounds."

Revie had been right to leave Albert out of a game that he thought would end up as a war of attrition with very little football played, although Albert didn't see it that way.

Albert was premature with his anger at being dropped as he only missed the one game, he was returned to the starting line-up for the following game against Cardiff City at the start of 1964.

Albert was putting in some great performances and was receiving a special support from home fans who had taken to him as 'one of our own'. But ironically many of the fans who were cheering Albert on would still go on to racially taunt any opposing black players, and the amount of racial abuse Albert faced at away games was still an obscene amount in a time of growing racial tension.

Migrant workers had become vital for the growth of Britain's economy and public services, but racism was on the rise. Previously there had been a 'colour bar' that prevented 'coloured' people obtaining jobs and accommodation and even fighting for British boxing titles.

Albert had settled in Leeds after initially saying: "I felt I would never get used to this new life. Many times I wished I had stayed at home."

Leeds United's record goalscorer Peter Lorimer, who signed for Leeds the year after Albert in 1962, said of Albert that early in his career at Leeds he would be invited to social events with the team, but he preferred not to attend and kept himself to himself.

The Leeds players tried to shield Albert from the abuse he would receive, and if any opposing team tried to intimidate Albert they would use the Leeds motto "side before self every time" to defend him.

Lorimer continued: "Our whole ethos was built on loyalty. All fight for each other, we all work for each other. If someone kicks me, he kicks all 11 of us."

Don Revie said of the Leeds approach in his early days as manager: "Maybe we did not endear ourselves to the soccer puritan... but we had to be realistic."

Leeds went into 1964 still top of the table and undaunted by the defeat to Sunderland. In their first game of the new year, they dug out a tough 1-0 victory away to Cardiff City in the F.A Cup before they gained revenge over high-flying Manchester City who had inflicted their first defeat of the season back in September. Leeds beat Man City 1-0 with Albert playing a pivotal role in the victory, Don Weston got the only goal of the game which gave Leeds the confidence to start believing that promotion was possible.

With confidence high Leeds would only lose one further league game in their seventeen remaining fixtures before the end of the season:

4/1/64 - Cardiff City away FA Cup 3rd round won 1-0 (Bremner) att 13,932,
11/1/64 - Manchester City home won 1-0 (Weston) att 33,737,
18/1/64 - Swindon Town away drew 2-2 (Giles, Hunter) att 19,015,
25/1/64 - Everton home FA Cup 4th round drew 1-1 (Lawson) att 48,826 (biggest crowd of the season in both league and cup).

Entering February 1964, Leeds sat in second place in the table and faced Welsh Cup winners Cardiff in the league at Elland Road. In a hard fought game Albert's explosive pace and bewitching side-step resulted in the only Leeds goal in a 1-1 draw, but Leeds were disappointed and felt it was a point dropped. Leeds next game continued their worst run of the season, although only losing once they drew the other four games for a five game winless run.

They got back to winning ways when Albert was the hero again when he hit the only goal in a tense game at home to Scunthorpe United in front of 28,868 fans:

1/2/64 - Cardiff City home drew 1-1 (Johanneson) att 28,039,
8/2/64 - Norwich City away drew 2-2 (Weston, Peacock) att 20,843,
15/2/64 - Scunthorpe United home won 1-0 (Johanneson) att 28,868,
22/2/64 - Huddersfield Town home drew 1-1 (Storrie) att 36,439.

March 1964 would see Leeds enter the month in second place and would see them lose only their third league game of the season on 3 March, when they were beaten by third placed Preston North End 2-0 away in front of 35,612 supporters. The defeat at Preston brought the two teams level for second place, two points behind Sunderland with Leeds having a better goal difference. The Preston defeat didn't faze Leeds though and Albert would score in the next game in a home win against high scoring Southampton 3-1 (Southampton scored 100 league goals in the 1963-64 season).

Leeds rallied themselves round and would go on to win four out of the five games they played in March. Albert starred in all the five games and scored in two of the wins. One of the goals came in the last match of March against a strong Newcastle side in front of a packed Elland Road, when 40,105 people turned up to see a goal that was described by everyone who saw it as a privilege to watch.

The memorable goal came in the third game that Leeds played in four days over the Easter period. After beating Newcastle away 1-0 in front of over 55,000 people on Friday 27 March, they then drew the following day with Derby County 1-1 at the Baseball Ground, before they faced Newcastle again on the Monday at Elland Road. In such a gruelling run of games and in such a crucial game, Albert's brilliance came to the fore by scoring the match-winning goal with fifteen minutes to go. Even the mercurial Johnny Giles said of Albert's goal: "Our second goal was scored by Johanneson and ranks as one of the most dazzling individual efforts I have ever seen. Albert was surrounded by three Newcastle defenders as he brought down a long pass through the middle and it all looked certain that he would be forced away from goal. Yet in the space of five yards, he side-stepped them all, one after the other, and nonchalantly slipped the ball past the goalkeeper as he came off his line. Albert was always such a nervous person off the field that it was unbelievable that he was capable of expressing himself like that on the field. That was his fifteenth goal of the season, the highest total by a Leeds winger since the war". Praise indeed from a magician like Giles. Albert's piece of sheer mastery had kept Leeds in the top spot and on course for promotion back to the first division:

3/3/64 - Preston North End away lost 2-0 att 35,612,

7/3/64 - Southampton won 3-1 (Johanneson, Lawson, Collins) att 24,077,

14/3/64 - Middlesbrough away won 3-1 (Lawson, Peacock, Giles) att 15,986,

21/3/64 - Grimsby Town home won 3-1 (Lawson, Peacock, Bremner) att 25,351

27/3/64 - Newcastle United away won 1-0 (Giles) att 55,038,

28/3/64 - Derby County away drew 1-1 (Peacock) att 16,757,

30/3/64 - Newcastle United home won 2-1 (Weston, Johanneson) 40,105.

After being in the top two since early December and with only four games to go, promotion was in their grasp. Leeds needed a minimum five points from a possible eight (2 points for a win in those days) as they had a far superior goal difference to Preston who were in third place. But with tricky games against relegation threatened Plymouth and Swansea the meticulous Don Revie was thorough in his final preparations.

Leeds actually managed to guarantee promotion with two games still left to play. Albert played in only two of the last four games due to injury, a 2-1 home win against Leyton Orient, and in the penultimate game of the season a 1-1 draw at home to Plymouth Argyle (a point which helped to keep Plymouth up on goal difference).

Leeds finished off a wonderful season with a 2-0 away win at Charlton Athletic, guaranteeing that they took the second division title, finishing two points above Sunderland. Leeds were returning to the top division after a four year absence with great optimism. Albert had played a major role in Leeds title winning success, playing in 37 games and scoring an impressive 15 goals. He had only missed five league games all season, two of which were in the final three games of the campaign.

The last two games of the season that Albert played in were:

4/4/64 - Leyton Orient home won 2-1 (Giles, Weston) att 30,920,

18/4/64 - Plymouth Argyle home drew 1-1 (Bell) att 34,725.

Leeds finished the 1963-64 season with 63 points, the highest total by a second division team since the Second World War. They had a twenty game unbeaten run which was their best since the 1927-28 season when they had finished runners-up in Division Two. They completed the season unbeaten at home for the very first time with 12 wins and 9 draws.

Albert had wrote himself into the history books and finished a great season finishing top scorer at Leeds with fifteen goals. He had featured in 41 games throughout the season in league (37) and cups (4) and appeared in front of crowds totalling over one million (1,045,695) paying customers, a far cry from his barefooted days with a tennis ball in South Africa.

Unfortunately, with the success, Leeds had gained a reputation as an 'ultra-aggressive' and a 'win-at-all-costs' side. There was no television coverage in those days which could counteract the claim by showing Albert's tricks or Johnny Giles' quality.

Although Leeds were an uncompromising side, a lot of the 1960s teams throughout all the leagues were built on aggression, but Leeds 'dirty' reputation was readily talked up by the press.

Don Revie's revolution was up and running and Albert had been a key figure in unlocking some of the more determined defences. His flair and speed complemented the gritty style Leeds often portrayed and in a lot of the tight games, he would open up even the most obdurate of teams.

With the average attendance at Elland Road over double what it was two seasons previous (29,938 1963-64 compared to 13,607 in 1961-62) Leeds were looking a force to be reckoned with.

Another feature of Leeds gaining promotion was a hit record. Leeds fan and pop star of the 1950s Ronnie Hilton penned a song called the *Leeds United Calypso*. Ronnie had a string of hits in the 50s including a number one ('No Other Love' 1956) and so with a West Indian tune and some questionable lyrics he celebrated Leeds promotion with the following song:

Leeds United calypso
Leeds United calypso
I feel so happy I feel so fine
The Elland Road lads are pals of mine (a-ha)
Now everybody come along with me
To Elland Road and sing joyfully
A lot of happy footballers you will see
The pride of the directors and Don Revie

It's the Leeds United calypso (sing it now)
Leeds United calypso
I feel so happy I feel so fine
The lads at Elland Road are pals of mine (a-ha)

Now matches have come and matches have gone
And at last we're happy in division one
Instead of the Mersey and Liverpool sound
We've got a special noise at the Elland Road ground

I feel so happy I feel so fine
The lads at Elland Road are buddies of mine (a-ha)

We've got Englishmen and Irishmen and Scotchmen, too

And our goallie called Sprake from Wales mark you

Albert Johanneson is one of the few

I don't know where he comes from, but I think it's Timbuctoo…

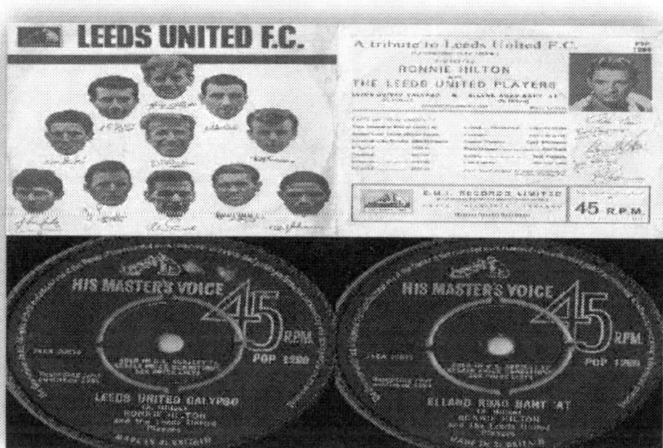

The song goes on, and apart from the ludicrous nature of the words the last verse gives a clear indication of the attitude at the time.

Photo: Ronnie Hilton and Don Revie

1964-1965 HISTORY TO BE MADE

Going into the 1964-65 season things were looking good for Albert, his career was booming and he had a settled family life. He had big hopes for the new season ahead.

Following Leeds promotion and their second division title triumph, Albert spent the summer back in South Africa for the first time in three years. Refreshed by the break, he was looking to rise to the challenge of top flight football in 1964-65.

Before the new season started a lot of critics were forecasting that Leeds would struggle in the top division and would face a relegation battle. But under Revie's guidance, their aggressive approach aligned with their teamwork and never-say-die attitude would soon quieten the critics. Albert's first taste of football in England's top flight would start very favourably. On 22 August 1964 in their first game back they found themselves a goal down after only four minutes away at Aston Villa. But they put in a resilient display and turned the game around to win 2-1.

Albert started in great form, scoring Leeds first goal of the new season, with Jack Charlton scoring the winner in front of a crowd of 28,000 at Villa Park. The newspaper report on the game said of Albert: "He settled down to his game probably faster than anybody on the field. He was tormenting Villa with his tricky running very quickly, and took his goal coolly from a fiery rebound off a vicious drive by Weston off goalkeeper Sidebottom."

Under Revie, Leeds had gained a reputation as a hard, cynical team which gave rise to the tag of 'Dirty Leeds'. The Football Association had released a report in the *FA News*, at the beginning of August 1964, which criticised the trend for poor discipline on the field. Leeds were named as the club with the poorest record in 1963-64 for players cautioned, censured, fined or suspended. Leeds defended its record by stating that the report was disingenuous in that it included the whole club including junior teams, and that the first teams' disciplinary record was no worse, if not better than any other league clubs. Revie defended his players by saying: "They are hard but fair, and I would not have it otherwise. Any player of mine must play hard. But we must get rid of this tag of dirty which I do not think the FA should have put upon us in their official magazine last week, and I shall be relieved if we get through the early season without trouble."
Unfortunately the die had been cast and there was trouble ahead.

Leeds second game of the season would be a big test at home against Liverpool who were reigning league champions. Liverpool had won the title in the second season after their own return to the big time. Leeds who had been buoyed by their opening day victory took the game to Liverpool, a team who had been described as 'full of thoroughbreds' and who were managed by the legendary Bill Shankly.

Leeds first game back at Elland Road in the top flight attracted a crowd of over thirty-six thousand to see Revie stick with the same eleven that played against Aston Villa. Don Weston continued to deputise for the injured Alan Peacock and he formed a twin spearhead with Jim Storrie, supplemented by the trickery of Albert and the guile of Johnny Giles on the wings.

The game marked a personal milestone for Albert as it was his one hundredth league game for Leeds United.

This particular game highlighted Leeds return to the big time and made the whole league sit up and take notice. Albert was central to the Leeds rise and was instrumental in the first goal when his shot from the edge of the 18-yard box hit Ron Yeats on the shoulder and kicked up under the bar to give Leeds a deserved lead. Leeds went on to record a memorable 4-2 win and had announced the start of what was to be a glorious era.

Albert was enjoying his football and things were going really well, in the third game of the season three days later at home, Leeds twice came from behind to record a 3-2 home win against Wolverhampton Wanderers in front of 34,538 crowd with Albert again in fine form and Elland Road was buzzing with excitement.

The great start was halted with the return fixture against Liverpool only a week after they had beaten them at Elland Road. In front of a crowd of 52,548 at Anfield, Leeds succumbed to their first defeat of the season losing 2-1. Although he was suffering from various niggling injuries, Albert continued to play. He got his second goal of the season when he scored in a 3-3 draw away at Sunderland in front of a crowd of 48,858, with the *Yorkshire Post* reporting that Albert: "Has so grown in confidence these days that he is now racing into the gaps and calling for the ball."

Leeds were brought down to earth in the next game, with a resounding 4-0 defeat at an Alan Ball inspired Blackpool. Ball would feature later in the Leeds story when Revie tried to sign him after the World Cup final in 1966. Ball alleged that he was given a £300 'bung' by Don Revie to reject Everton's approach for his services and request that the Blackpool chairman sell him to Leeds instead. Needless-to-say, both Leeds United and Revie strenuously denied that any such thing had ever happened, but that didn't prevent the Football Association from later charging both Revie and Ball (who claimed to have pocketed the 'bung') with bringing the game into disrepute. The FA fined Ball £3,000, even though he had ended up at Everton, and not Revie's Leeds. Revie didn't receive a fine.

Leeds bounced back in the next 2 games with Albert scoring in the 3-2 win at home to Leicester City and starring in the reverse fixture against Blackpool, exacting revenge with a 3-0 win to take them up to second in the table.

22/8/64 - Aston Villa away won 2-1 (Johanneson, Charlton) att 28,000,
26/8/64 - Liverpool home won 4-2 (Yeats og, Weston, Bremner, Giles) att 36,005,
29/8/64 - Wolverhampton Wanderers home won 3-2 (Storrie 2, Charlton) att 34,538,
2/9/64 - Liverpool away lost 2-1 (Collins) att 52,548,
5/9/64 - Sunderland away drew 3-3 (Storrie, Bell, Johanneson) att 48,858,
7/9/64 - Blackpool away lost 4-0 att 26,310,
12/9/64 - Leicester City home won 3-2 (Bremner 2 - 1 pen, Johanneson) att 32,300,
16/9/64 - Blackpool home won 3-0 (Collins 2, |Hunter) att 35,973.

After playing eight games in twenty-five days, Leeds were flying high and Albert was in the form of his life. Their next fixture was the toughest they faced so far, away at unbeaten table toppers Chelsea. The clash of the top two ended in a 2-0 win for Chelsea, resulting in Leeds dropping down to eighth in the table.

The report in the *Yorkshire Evening Post* summed up Leeds' approach to life in the top division saying: 'It was all hurry and scurry at breakneck speed, with little time for finesses, invention or the unexpected: the ball was passed incessantly crossfield or backwards in an effort to unhinge packed defensive covering. Both sides resembled a terrier scurrying the length of a hedge in search of a gap. 'Never mind the ball' seemed to be the order of the day as scything, irresponsible tackles ruffled tempers. The midget Collins once retaliated on Harris viciously and had his name taken when he might well have been despatched to the dressing room to ponder his action; McCreadie hooked up Giles painfully and, with half an hour gone, left Leeds permanently reduced to 10 men as the wounded winger was carried away from the scene on a stretcher.'

This was in the days before any substitutes were allowed so players would often carry on even if they were injured.

These were not the type of games that Albert would normally be able to shine in, but he dug deep and continued with his stylish way of playing.

He was rested for the mid-week League Cup win over Huddersfield but was back in the side for the 2-1 home defeat to Nottingham Forest three days later. After two consecutive defeats Leeds had dropped down to the lowest position they would be in all season - eleventh. After a 2-2 draw at home to Fulham, Leeds got back to winning ways with a 3-2 away win at Stoke City. Albert was back on the scoresheet again but the goal came in a 3-2 defeat at home to Aston Villa in the League Cup fourth round.

19/9/64 - Chelsea away lost 2-0 att 38,006

26/9/64 - Nottingham Forest home lost 2-1 (Storrie) att 32,776,

30/9/64 - Fulham home drew 2-2 (Storrie 2) att 31,260,

10/10/64 - Stoke City away won 3-2 (Storrie 2, Greenhoff) att 27,561,

14/10/64 - Aston Villa home League Cup Rd 3 lost 3-2 (Johanneson, Collins) att 10,656.

The General Election in October 1964 highlighted some of the growing racism in Britain. In Smethwick it was alleged that the Conservative candidate, Peter Griffiths, who would go on to be elected to Parliament, ran on the slogan: "If you want a nigger as a neighbour, vote Liberal or Labour." Although the party disassociated itself from the comment, Griffiths said: "I would not condemn any man who said that. I regard it as a manifestation of popular feeling." It prompted International Civil Rights Campaigner, Malcolm X to visit Smethwick on February 12 1965 to advocate for desegregated housing in Smethwick. Unfortunately Malcolm X didn't live long enough to see if his plea would come to fruition as he was gunned down in Manhattan's Audubon Ballroom 9 days later on February 21, 1965. With such mainstream racism apparent, it highlights the battle that Albert and his contemporaries would face on a daily basis.

Having beaten Stoke in their last league game, Leeds would win the next six league games to take them up from seventh to third in the table, with only Manchester United (4 points) and Chelsea (1 point) above them. Albert would play in all the six victories, scoring in the 4-1 win against Sheffield United. After beating Tottenham, Burnley and Sheffield United,

Leeds travelled to play an Everton side that were two points behind them in the table at Goodison Park. The game became known as the 'The battle of Goodison' and was described by one newspaper reporter as 'a spine chilling encounter'. On 7 November 1964, from the opening seconds of the game, the match brimmed over with grudging aggression. After only five minutes Everton full-back Sandy Brown was sent off for punching Johnny Giles in the stomach after Giles had left stud marks on the full back's chest.

In front of a crowd of 43,065 the game soon reached boiling point after Willie Bell opened the scoring for Leeds. After 38 minutes, for the first time in English league football, the hostility was such that the referee took both teams off the field in an attempt to calm the players and fans down. Willie Bell and Derek Temple were still laid out on the pitch after a clash of heads with Bell saying of the incident: "I was dazed by the collision and when I came to, Les Cocker, Giles and Storrie were the only other men left on the pitch. I thought I was dreaming! During the break, which lasted nearly ten minutes, Revie told us to keep our heads, and naturally all the lads started talking about Everton's tactics. Albert Johanneson claimed someone was calling him a black bastard and Revie joked: "Call him a white bastard then!" That relieved the tension a bit, but the game itself got out of hand again. It was absolutely frightening. From the kick off, Jack Charlton booted the ball upfield and one of Everton's players came right through and kicked him. It got so bad that one of our players spent most of the match watching the clock, hoping for the game to end! The crowd baited us from the start while Everton appeared to have an obsession about gaining the edge over us, physically. We couldn't help but get involved."

As the physio's worked on the injured players they came under a barrage of objects and the referee, Ken Stokes was hit by a coin. At that point the official made a decision unprecedented in English football - he halted the game. Brown had been sent off, Bell was carried off, Temple was stretchered off and in the end it all kicked off! With the crowd up in arms, Billy Bremner was confronted by a fan as he left the pitch with Goodison in uproar. When play resumed after the calming period, the rough play and heavy tackles continued. The game finished with Leeds running out 1-0 winners and the police had to clear the streets around Goodison after the game. For someone of a delicate nature the game shook Albert, and it was said that he was in tears when he came off at the end of the game. One surprising aspect of such a rough game was that apart from the sending off there was only one booking, when in the view of the reporter Norman Hunter was unluckily booked for a tackle on Everton forward Roy Vernon.

Photo: Billy Bremner in the middle of a ruck on a muddy pitch…a regular feature of games involving Leeds in the 1960s

The Football League held a meeting over the 'Battle of Goodison' with the League president Joe Richards saying: "Something must be done and we must find out the cause. Competition is very healthy but things seem to be getting too keen. It could be because players are getting too much money for points."

Richards was referring to the abolition of the £20 maximum wage after players had threatened to strike in 1961. On 9 December 1964, the League committee responded to the game by suspending Everton's Sandy Brown for two weeks for his sending off and fined Everton £250 for the behaviour of their fans. Leeds came out unscathed, although their reputation was tarnished even further.

Leeds United and Wales goalkeeper throughout the 1960s and early 1970s was Gary Sprake. He gave his opinion on Albert in the book 'Careless Hands': "I remember Albert as a very skilful player. He had great ball control with electrifying pace and could also score goals. He was shy and nervous both on and off the pitch but was a great favourite with the Elland Road faithful. When we played away however, he unfortunately suffered racial abuse from a small minority. The worst I witnessed was a game at Goodison Park. They were making monkey noises and some idiots threw bananas at Albert. As you can imagine he was extremely upset and being a timid person it affected him deeply. Even though players used to wind each other up during games, opposing players never once made racist remarks towards him (a claim Albert would totally disagree with). I think it was a terrible shame the way some fans treated him as Albert was a very nice man."

Although the Everton game had left a mark on Albert he still pulled himself together for the next game at home to Arsenal in front of 38,620 supporters which Leeds won 3-1. With Albert's skill and agility playing such a pivotal role Don Revie insisted: "His men can, and will, play good football if they are allowed." The *Yorkshire Post* noted that Albert: "Has so grown in confidence these days that he is now racing into the gaps and calling for the ball."

17/10/64 - Tottenham Hotspur home won 3-1 att 41,464,
24/10/64 - Burnley away won 1-0 (Bell) att 24,329,
31/10/64 - Sheffield United home won 4-0 (Collins, Storrie, Johanneson, Belfitt) att 33,357,
7/11/64 - Everton away won 1-0 (Bell) att 43,605,
11/11/64 - Arsenal home won 3-1 (Charlton, Belfitt, Storrie) att 38,620,
14/11/64 - Birmingham City home won 4-1 (Storrie, Charlton, Collins, Giles) att 32,030.

After beating Birmingham 4-1 at Elland Road to chalk up a seventh consecutive win - Leeds were now third, a point behind Chelsea and two behind leaders Manchester United. Albert was causing havoc for defences with his dazzling runs and crosses from the left flank. He had started in the first eighteen games of the season but injury ruled him out of the next three games. Although flying high, Leeds came a cropper without Albert in the side, away at seventh place West Ham United losing 3-1. After the West Ham defeat Leeds went on a 25 game unbeaten run which included three FA Cup games. Albert made his return in a 1-0 win home win against

Aston Villa on 12 December 1964 in front of the lowest league home crowd of the season (27,339) and he played in four consecutive games, scoring in one of them, before injury struck ruling him out of a home fixture against Sunderland:

12/12/64 - Aston Villa home won 1-0 (Lee og) att 27,399,
19/12/64 - Wolverhampton Wanderers away won 1-0 (Johnson) att 17,126,
26/12/64 - Blackburn Rovers home drew 1-1 (Storrie) att 45,341,
28/12/64 - Blackburn Rovers away won 2-0 (Storrie, Johanneson) att 24,511.

Although Albert didn't play in the Sunderland game, the 2-1 win took Leeds to the top of the first division for the first time in their history, an achievement that would become a regular feature under Don Revie. They sat at the top of division one, two points above both Chelsea and Manchester United, although both of those teams had a game in hand on Leeds.

Leeds United had never reached an FA Cup Final since it was formed in 1919, but hopes were high at Elland Road with their current run of form instilling a new found confidence. Their FA Cup journey got off to a good start on the 9 January 1965 when they beat fourth division Southport 3-0 at home. In the end it was a comfortable victory but the contest wasn't over until Albert scored the second goal in the 81st minute.

Two 2-2 draws followed in the league against Leicester and Chelsea which kept Leeds at the top of the table before they faced Everton for the first time since the 'Battle of Goodison' in the FA Cup 4th round.

A 1-1 draw at home was played out in front of 50,051 supporters on 30 January, after the draw Leeds thought they had blown their chance of progressing. The game had been another physical encounter which saw Albert getting injured and forcing him to miss the replay at Goodison Park three days later. In the replay, Leeds turned in a great performance to come away with a 2-1 win in front of a crowd of 65,940.

Albert also missed the following two league fixtures, a 0-0 draw away at Nottingham Forest and a 2-1 win away at Arsenal. He did make a return in the 2-0 win against Shrewsbury Town in the fifth round of the FA Cup on 20 February in front of a crowd of 47,740 at Elland Road. Albert finished the game off with the second goal after Johnny Giles had opened the scoring from the penalty spot.

9/1/65 - Southport FA Cup 3rd Round home won 3-0 (Greenhoff, Johanneson, Johnson) att 31,297,
16/1/65 - Leicester City away drew 2-2 (Charlton, Johnson) att 23,230,
23/1/65 - Chelsea home drew 2-2 (Storrie, Charlton) att 47,109,
30/1/65 - Everton home drew 1-1 (Storrie) att 50,051,
20/2/65 - Shrewsbury Town FA Cup 5th Round home won 2-0 (Giles pen, Johanneson) att 47,740.

Albert then played in a 0-0 draw away at Tottenham the following week where he was injured again causing him to miss the next two away games against Crystal Palace and Fulham. With Leeds still second in the table, Albert made a scoring return in a 5-1 demolition of Burnley at Elland Road on 15 March. The next game was the return league game against Everton at Elland Road following the 'Battle of Goodison' in November. Albert noted that this was one of his favourite games. He said some of the Everton players were calling him 'nig-nog' and 'golliwog' as soon as they arrived at the ground. Don Revie again told Albert to not listen to them and just ignore them. Seeking advice from the inspirational Billy Bremner, Billy told Albert to: "Use their negativity against them and get stuck into them, show them up for what they are – useless."

Albert said he took Billy's advice and had a tremendous game, ripping Everton apart and scoring twice in a resounding 4-1 win, which took Leeds back to the top of the table. In the four games that Leeds played against Everton in the 1964-65 season the total attendances for the four games was 189,297, and although Albert thrilled in the atmosphere of big games, the constant abuse he received was affecting him quite badly. Billy Bremner said of the abuse: "Many times during a game Albert would devastate teams with his blistering pace and finishing. Some of the racial abuse he would get from opposition players and fans was disgraceful. I would try and protect him from that and so would the rest of the lads."

The Everton game on 20 March 1965 was also notable as the first ever televised Leeds United home game which raised the profile of the players even more. The television recording shows Albert scoring the first and third goals in grainy black and white pictures. The stadium was snow swept and the pitch was muddy and uneven, making Albert's performances even the more remarkable. TV broadcaster, Keith Macklin said of Albert: "When I saw him racing down the wing with the ball, I thought, this lad has magic in his feet."

27/2/65 - Tottenham Hotspur away drew 0-0 att 42,202,

15/3/65 - Burnley home won 5-1 (Collins 2, Charlton 2, Johanneson) att 38,506,

20/3/65 - Everton home won 4-1 (Johanneson 2, Bremner, Peacock) att 29,701.

Leeds had a hectic finale to the season having to play eleven games in thirty-five days, one of which was an FA Cup semi-final (and replay) which eventually led to their first FA Cup Final appearance.

They also had eight league games left which would decide where the league title would go. They were involved in a three-way battle with Chelsea and Manchester for the chance of their very first top flight league title.

On 27 March they faced arch rivals Manchester United in the FA Cup semi-final in front of 60,000 fans at Hillsborough in bitterly fought contest.

Albert was a marked man and Nobby Stiles took him out with a dreadful tackle early on which restricted his mobility and would force him to miss the replay. Eric Stranger reported on the game in the *Yorkshire Evening Post* saying: 'Perhaps it is as well there is a replay at Nottingham on Wednesday. At least it will give both sides opportunity to show that they can play good football and redeem themselves for a shabby, bitter FA Cup semi-final at Hillsborough on Saturday. There were no goals but there were 24 free kicks for fouls given against Manchester United and 10 against Leeds. Two Manchester players, Stiles and Law, had their names taken and altogether too many players on both sides behaved like a pack of dogs snapping and snarling at each other over a bone.'

27/3/65 - Manchester United FA Cup Semi-Final (neutral Hillsborough) drew 0-0 att 65,000.

Photo: Leeds v Manchester United strong rivalry on 1960s muddy pitches

Terry Cooper replaced Albert in the replay with the report saying of his absence: 'it was due to the bloody minded assaults on Johanneson at the weekend.'

The epic 1-0 replay win was decided when Billy Bremner scored an 89th minute winner and meant that Leeds had reached the FA Cup Final for the first time in their history.

With seven games left of the season the title chase had been whittled down to three dominant teams: Chelsea, Leeds and Manchester United.

There was no time to celebrate the semi-final win though as they faced West Ham in the league three days later at Elland Road. Albert would miss five league games due to the injury he received in the semi-final including two consecutive defeats, one against Manchester United at home (1-0) and the other away at Sheffield Wednesday (3-0). The defeat put Leeds third in the table, one point behind Manchester United (57 points) who had three games to play, and on the same points as Chelsea (56 points) who had played a game more (40 games). Albert returned for the return fixture against Sheffield Wednesday which remarkably was played the next day. This meant that Leeds had to play three games in four days in their title run in. Leeds avenged the 3-0 defeat with Albert starring in a 2-0 home win.

Leeds then played their third game against a team from Sheffield in a four day period, this time beating Sheffield United away 3-0.

With one league match remaining it was a mighty tall order for Leeds to win the title. They travelled to play Birmingham City in a Monday night fixture, their fifth match in 10 days on 26 April 1965. Going into the last game of the season, Leeds were one point clear of Manchester United who still had two games to play and had a better goal difference.

Birmingham City were already relegated and doomed to finish bottom of the table. By this time Albert was still self-deprecating and vulnerable, and as his profile had heightened, he had become more of a known quantity, and consequently a marked man. He played in his thirtieth game of an arduous first division campaign at Birmingham, although things didn't go as planned as Birmingham were three goals up without reply ten minutes into the second half. Even though Leeds had the FA Cup final to come five days later they weren't giving up the league without making a last gasp effort. Goals from Giles (penalty) and Paul Reaney's first ever league goal put them back in the game, and when Jack Charlton equalised two minutes from time the impossible looked on. Leeds kept pressing for a winner that would give them a chance of their first league title and a possible double, but their luck ran out when Norman Hunter crashed the ball against the post in injury time. To make matters worse Albert picked up a knock in the game which would hamper him for the FA Cup final 5 days later. Leeds lost out in the league to Manchester United on goal difference with both teams finishing on sixty-one points, five ahead of Chelsea.

20/4/65 - Sheffield Wednesday home won 2-0 (Storrie, Giles pen) att 45,065,

24/4/65 - Sheffield United away won 3-0 (Storrie, Bremner, Peacock) att 32,928,

26/4/65 - Birmingham City away drew 3-3 (Giles pen, Reaney, Charlton) att 16,644.

Albert's first taste of football in the top division had gone well, he played in thirty league games scoring nine goals (twelve in total for the season), and said of the challenge: "I really enjoyed playing in that first season in division one. Our resilience was tested each week, and we showed with our football that we were able to challenge with the best players in the game."

There was a bandwagon of people who said with hindsight after Albert's career had finished that he wasn't able to 'handle it' in the first division and that he was just a brilliant second division player. But his performances in a season when Leeds would just miss out on the title on goal difference and reach an FA Cup final would suggest otherwise. He contributed almost a goal every three games from a wide position and he came in for the brunt of brutality from opposing teams. As George Best said: "He was brave to take the field in the first place. People said I was good, but Albert had far more skill and pace than I had, he left me breathless at times."

Although just missing out on the league title, Leeds season wasn't finished. They had the matter of playing in their first ever FA Cup final against Bill Shankley's legendary Liverpool team only five days after the 3-3 draw at Birmingham. On May 1, 1965, Albert would make history by being the first ever non-white player to appear in the FA Cup final in front of 100,000 fans. Albert enjoyed the week leading up to the final saying it was one of the best weeks of his life with all the press attention, praise and fan approval. He said: "I enjoyed the thrill of being recognised for being a footballer and the style and lifestyle that brings complimentary meals in restaurants, free drinks, countless compliments and much adulation."

But on the day of the final things turned sour. He said that he felt his self-confidence drain from him when he heard a journalist refer to him as 'sambo'. He overheard the journalist say: "If he plays, he will be the first ever black footballer to play in a Cup Final at Wembley. Who would have thought it? A man raised in filthy rat-infested slums now playing in an FA Cup Final."

Albert's insecurities came flooding back and fear overtook him, he was left feeling like he didn't want to play in the biggest game of his career. He approached Don Revie and asked him to withdraw him from the game, but Revie didn't want to hear from him saying:

"You don't want to play because someone has called you a stupid bloody name? I'm not listening to you, you are capable of winning this game for us, that's why you are playing."

Although Revie meant it as a compliment and to encourage him, it didn't ease Albert worries. He said his whole body was trembling and he spent most of the time before the game in the bathroom with diarrhoea and being sick. As the teams were led out by Revie and Shankly the crowd of 100,000 went crazy with excitement. Albert didn't feel the excitement, just fear, he said: "When we walked out, all I could hear was a cacophony of Zulu-like noises coming from the terraces. It was dreadful, I could barely hear myself think for those screams. I wanted to run back down the tunnel."

But as bad as the noise was, Albert said he just tried to fill his mind with how proud his family and friends would be at seeing him play at Wembley.

The difference in the mental attitude was there for all to see, as the teams were led out onto the pitch in front of millions on television and a sell-out crowd in attendance. There was a stark difference between Billy Bremner looking confident and assured, juggling the ball on his head as he strutted out, compared to Albert who had a hunched walk with what looked like the world on his shoulders.

Leeds 1965 FA Cup Final Team:

1. Gary Sprake
2. Paul Reaney
3. Willie Bell
4. Billy Bremner
5. Jack Charlton
6. Norman Hunter
7. Johnny Giles
8. Jim Storrie
9. Alan Peacock
10. Bobby Collins
11. Albert Johanneson

The game itself was played on a heavy, muddy pitch and turned out to be an anti-climax. The press who had initially described it as the 'War of the Roses' afterwards reported it as the 'Bore of the Roses'. Liverpool ran out deserved 2-1 winners with all three goals coming in extra time. It was Liverpool's first FA Cup final win in their history.

Of the result, Bill Shankly wrote in his autobiography: "Grown men were crying, and it was the greatest feeling any human being could have to see what we have done."

It was a different story for Albert, he had made his own history that day but had a different outlook to that of Shankly's. He said he looked back on the occasion 'with much despair and sadness' and if he had the chance to do things again, it is the one event he would go back and change. Through his despair he was unable to see the ground-breaking achievement he had made in being the first non-white player in the ninety-three-year history of the FA Cup to play in the final. He failed to see the advancement he had made for black players everywhere.

Photo: Albert in the pre match line up after shaking hands with Prince Phillip.

Such was Albert's low esteem that he took the defeat and his performance to heart. He felt he had let everyone down who'd ever known him, and although Les Cocker tried to reassure him with the prospect of further Wembley appearances, Albert had felt that the damage had been done, and he also felt that his relationship with Revie would never the be the same due to the events before the game.

1/5/65 – Liverpool FA Cup Final Wembley lost 2-1 aet (Bremner) att 100,000.

Ken Jones of *The Daily Mirror* reported on the game:
"Discipline was destroyed by tiredness, determination blunted by the pain of having to run some more. Behind the boredom was the failure of individuals like Leeds left winger Albert Johanneson and Liverpool left winger Peter Thompson, men who could and should have lifted the game with their talent."

After previously spending three seasons before their promotion struggling in the second division, Leeds return to the top flight had been a major success. Runners-up in both the League and FA Cup should have been seen as a magnificent success but it felt like a disappointment with no silverware. The press had seemingly delighted in the fact that 'Dirty Leeds' had ended the season empty handed. Liverpool manager, Bill Shankly responded to the question as to whether Leeds had failed by saying: "Failed? Second in the championship. Cup finalists. Ninety percent of managers would pray for 'failures' like that."

Despite no silverware, the future was looking very promising for this new young vibrant Leeds side under the guidance of Harry Reynolds and

Don Revie. Reynolds had backed Revie unconditionally and although the youth policy was paying dividends, if Revie wanted a player Reynolds would go all out to get that player.

Attendances were on the up again from an average of 28,723 in 1963-64 to 36,413 in 1964-65, an improvement of over 23,000 from when Revie took over as manager in 1961.

Although Albert played in fewer games in the 1964-65 season (36) as opposed to the 1963-64 season (41), due to the increase in attendances in the first division and the large crowds for FA Cup games, Albert played in front of the most people he would face in a single season 1,335,398.

Albert returned to South Africa for the summer to reflect on the season just passed and to help him cope with the disappointment of the cup final. He was worried about how his cup final performance would affect his future at Leeds and hoped that some South African sunshine and family time would recharge his batteries for the new season ahead.

Although he had disappointed in the cup final itself and was distraught with his own performance, the mere fact that he had achieved what no other black player had done previously should have given him an immense amount of satisfaction. He had showed that any black child watching could see that it was possible for them to reach the pinnacle of English football just as Albert had.

Albert hadn't forgot his roots and where he came from. After the cup final he gifted his match shirt to Barney Gaffney the schoolteacher scout who had coached him and had made it possible for him to come over to England.

FIRST BLACK PLAYER TO SCORE IN AN FA CUP FINAL - MICHAEL TREBILCOCK

Photo: FA Cup hero Mike Trebilcock crowned with the FA Cup

After Albert's historic albeit disappointing appearance in the 1965 FA Cup Final, it wasn't long before the next black player would play in football's prestigious event. After waiting ninety-three years for the first appearance, Mike Trebilcock followed Albert into an FA Cup final the following year - with greater success. In the Cup Final of 1966, Everton faced Sheffield Wednesday on 14 May 1966 at Wembley.

Everton had reached the final by beating both Manchester sides. Manchester City in an epic quarter final which took three games to decide (0-0, 0-0 and 2-0) and a semi-final win over Manchester United (1-0).

Trebilcock was described as a 'black mixed heritage player' who had joined Everton in December 1965 from Plymouth Argyle. Unfortunately his career at Everton was curtailed almost straight away through injury.

He recovered in time for the FA Cup Final but he wasn't expected to play, and wasn't even featured in the match day programme. But as fate would have it, with an injury to first choice striker Fred Pickering, manager Harry Catterick threw Trebilcock in at the deep end and he made the starting eleven.

As the game went on it looked like it was going to end in failure for Trebilcock and Everton when Sheffield Wednesday took a two-goal lead after fifty-seven minutes. But only two minutes later Trebilcock made history when on fifty-nine minutes, he became the first non-white footballer to score in an FA Cup Final. The second goal wasn't far behind when he caused pandemonium amongst the Everton fans when he equalised five minutes later (64th minute) by hammering the ball home from the edge of the penalty area.

And, with only 16 minutes remaining, Gerry Young in the Sheffield Wednesday defence failed to control a bouncing ball, allowing Derek Temple to race clear and fire past the Wednesday goalkeeper Ron Springett from the edge of the area to put Everton ahead for the first time. Trebilcock had a chance to mark his fairytale by completing his hat-trick - which would have been only the second one in FA Cup Final history after Stan Mortensen in 1953 - shortly after but was denied by the Springett.

Due to his heroics in the cup final, Trebilcock would become an Everton legend even though he only ever played a total of fourteen games in his three-year Everton career.

After the glory of the FA Cup Final he struggled to establish himself in the Everton side and in January 1968, after three goals in only 11 league games for Everton, he moved to Portsmouth for a fee of £40,000.

He was a regular goal scorer at Portsmouth, netting 33 times in 109 league games, and scored three goals in four games on loan to Torquay United, before a free transfer took him to Weymouth in 1973. He eventually finished his career in Australia at Western Suburbs.

Trebilcock was just twenty-four when he signed for Everton from Plymouth Argyle, which was a dream move for a player who had been playing for non-League Tavistock just a couple of years earlier.

Although his transfer from Plymouth Argyle to Everton was a major career move, it came with some heartache though as it was such a sudden move that he had to end his relationship with his girlfriend, Ginny.

Trebilcock explains: “I was home one night from the movies not knowing my manager was about to knock on the door and tell me I was going to Liverpool in the morning,”

“I didn’t even have time to tell my family or any of my team mates at Argyle. “It was tough, I didn’t think I’d ever see Ginny again. I never forgot her though, you never forget your first love.”

There was to be a happy ending to the story when the childhood sweethearts were re-united in 2016 after over 50 years apart. They found the love was still there and decided to finally get married and settle back in Tavistock.

Trebilcock said: “I feel blessed at being given this chance of happiness. I finally got her – it took me 52 years, but I got her.”

BILL PERRY FA CUP HERO

William (Bill) Perry (1930-2007), was the son of an English man and a South African woman. He was born in Johannesburg on 10th September, 1930. He played outside-left and joined Johannesburg Rangers in 1946.

Although of mixed parentage Perry identified as white, otherwise he would have taken the honour of being the first non-white player to appear in and score in an FA Cup Final. He would also have been the first player to be capped by England.

He was described as dark skinned, but like a lot of white South Africans, culturally and racially he was termed as 'white'.

Perry scored the winning goal in the 1951 FA Cup semi-final replay for Blackpool against Birmingham City at Everton's Goodison Park, but they would go on to be beaten by Newcastle United 2-0 in the final.

Not to be denied, Blackpool reached the FA Cup Final for the third time in six years in 1953.

The 1953 final became known as the 'Matthews Final' in honour of the great Stanley Matthews. Matthews inspired his team to come from 3–1 down against Bolton Wanderers, to win 4–3, to claim the trophy that had so far eluded him in his magnificent career.

The game is one of the all-time classics. Bolton had taken a 3-1 lead early in the second half, but then Stan Mortensen scored from a Matthews cross. Matthews said of the goal: "Although under pressure from two Bolton defenders who contrived to whack him from either side as he slid in, his determination was total and he managed to toe poke the ball off the inside of the post and into the net."

Then in the 88th minute a Bolton defender conceded a free kick approximately 20 yards from goal. Stan Mortensen took the kick and according to Matthews: "Such was the power and accuracy behind Morty's effort, Hanson in the Bolton goal hardly moved a muscle."

Stanley Matthews described in his autobiography what happened next: "A minute of injury time remained... Ernie Taylor, who had not stopped running throughout the match, picked up a long throw from George Farm, rounded Langton and, as he had done like clockwork through the second half, found me wide on the right. I took off for what I knew would be one final run to the byline. Three Bolton players closed in, I jinked past Ralph Banks and out of the corner of my eye noticed Barrass coming in quick for the kill. They had forced me to the line and it was pure instinct that I pulled the ball back to where experience told me Morty would be. In making the cross I slipped on the greasy turf and, as I fell, my heart and hopes fell also. I looked across and saw that Morty, far from being where I expected him to be, had peeled away to the far post. We could read each other like books. For five years we'd had this understanding. He knew exactly where I'd put the ball. Now, in this game of all games, he wasn't there. This was our last chance, what on earth was he doing? Racing up from deep into the space was Bill Perry." Matthews added that Perry "coolly and calmly stroked the ball wide of Hanson and Johnny Ball on the goal line and into the corner of the net."

Bill Perry described his goal: "Whenever Stan (Matthews) got the ball, all the forwards made for the goalmouth because nine times out of ten, Stan would beat his full-back and we knew the ball would be coming across. That is what I anticipated and sure enough, Stan got the ball on the wing, and crossed it, although he slipped as he did so, meaning he cut it back a little sharper than he had meant to. Morty let it go by at the near post as he wasn't in a good position and it came to me along the ground. It was just about on the penalty spot when I let fly with my right foot and I was so glad to see it hit the back of the net. For the first time in the match, we were ahead and we knew then that the Cup was ours. It was a marvellous moment and one I will never forget."

But such was Matthews influence and brilliance, even though Stan Mortensen scored a hat-trick (still the only ever FA Cup Final hat-trick) that day and Bill Perry scored a ninety-second minute winner, the final still became known as the 'Matthews Final'.

Perry would go on to play for England against Northern Ireland on 1st November, 1955, with England winning the game 3-1.

In his next game for his country, Perry scored two of the goals in England's 4-1 win over Spain, and he won his last cap against Scotland on 14th April 1956.

During his time at Blackpool Perry scored 119 goals in 394 games. He also went on to play for Southport and Hereford United.

PETER FOLEY MBE

Another story of the effect of racism in the 1960s was the story of Peter Foley. The son of a white mother and black father, Peter Foley was born in Edinburgh on 28th June 1944, and became the first professional black footballer from Cumbria.

He was one of the few black players to play in the football league in the 1960s, and on 5 April 1965 while playing for Workington against Queen's Park Rangers in London, Peter faced his first episode of racism which affected him deeply. Chants of "Zulu, Zulu, Zulu" came from the small but vociferous Queens Park Rangers supporters which he knew was aimed at him as the only black player on the pitch. The chants had a profound effect on Peter and played on his mind.

With the trauma from Queen's Park Rangers game still fresh in his mind, upon seeing that the first fixture for the following season was again in London against Millwall who were known for their notorious following, Peter feigned injury so he wouldn't have to travel to London.

Feeling that he had let himself and his team down, Peter said he used the experience as a valuable lesson and vowed never to let such an incident affect him in a negative way ever again. He would go on to use the experience as an incentive to fight racism wherever he could.

Peter stated that there was a distinct lack of diversity in his playing days and that in his six-year football league career from 1965 to 1971 with Workington, Scunthorpe and Chesterfield he never played in a team with another black player or indeed saw another black player in an opposition team.

Peter has received several honours for his work against racism.

In 1998 he received an award for his work as well as being a 'Pioneer of Black British Football' from the Professional Footballers' Association.

He was awarded an MBE in the New Year's Honour's list in 2003 for his anti-racism work especially on the 'Let's Kick Racism Out of Football' campaign and was admitted to the 'Show Racism the Red Card' Hall of Fame in 2013 which was established in January 1996 for his sterling work on their campaign.

ALBERT 1965-66 – FA CUP AFTERMATH

At the start of the new season the popular opinion in the press was that Leeds would be one season wonders. The view was that their hard working and at times abrasive style of play would be figured out and counteracted by opposing sides.

The 1965-66 season was notable for the use of substitutes for the first time in football league history. The ruling was limited though as there was only one substitute to be named and they could only be used in the case of an injury.

Albert's fears about his reaction in the cup final affecting his place in the team were realised when he was replaced in the starting eleven at the start of the 1965-66 season by the exciting new talent of Terry Cooper. Cooper would go on to make his name at left-back but started his career in Albert's position on the left wing.

Leeds started the season well with two victories. A 1-0 win at home to Sunderland and a 2-0 away win at Aston Villa. Albert's first start of the season came in the fourth game after Leeds had been beaten 2-1 at West Ham.

He played well in a 2-0 home win over Aston Villa which took Leeds to the top of the table defying the critics from the start of the season who thought they would struggle.

Albert retained his place in the 2-1 win at home against Nottingham Forest. Things were starting to look good for Leeds and Albert, but a 3-2 defeat at Tottenham and a 2-2 draw at home to Sheffield United dropped Leeds down to sixth in the table, their lowest position all season.

Albert played in the next game, a 2-0 home win against Tottenham but would miss the following twenty-one games, including Leeds very first game in Europe a 2-1 win over Torino in front of 33,852 supporters at Elland Road. Albert could only watch on as Billy Bremner scored their very first European goal in the Inter-City Fairs Cup, with Alan Peacock scoring the second.

1/9/65 - Aston Villa home won 2-0 (Peacock 2) att 33,575,
4/9/65 - Nottingham Forest home won 2-1 (Bell, Lorimer) att 35,427,
8/9/65 - Tottenham Hotspur away lost 3-2 (Lorimer, Clayton og) att 48,114,
11/9/65 - Sheffield United home drew 2-2 (Bremner, Hunter) att 33,249,
15/9/65 - Tottenham Hotspur home won 2-0 (Bremner, Charlrton) att 41,920.

Albert felt that he was becoming a fringe player in the 1965-66 season, a feeling compounded when he was substituted in both the Sheffield United and Tottenham games. Leeds also signed the highly rated left-winger, Mike O'Grady for £30,000 from Huddersfield Town in October 1965, a signing which gave Albert's already low self-esteem a further knock.

By now he said the communication between himself and Revie had become almost non-existent, with Revie only acknowledging Albert when he was in the first team or when he was in the treatment room. His position wasn't helped with the club telling the press that the reason for his non-selection was due to injuries which he denied was the case. The lack of first team opportunities began to weigh heavy on Albert.

It was around this time that he said he took the first steps to oblivion. He took up smoking, which he said was a common practice among players in the changing rooms in those days. But even worse was that he started to drink 'maybe once or twice a week' to help him relax.

But as his first team appearances became less and less, he became more anxious and started to drink every day. He admitted that he was squandering money, and his health, performance and domestic life suffered as a consequence. The vicious circle had started. The more games he missed the more he drank, and the more he drank the more his fitness suffered.

Albert wouldn't make a reappearance in the first team until 15 January 1966 when he featured in the 2-2 draw at home to Stoke City. He retained his place in a 6-0 home demolition of Bury in the FA Cup third round. With Leeds fourth in the table Albert played in his seventh league game of the season the following week in a 2-0 league defeat away to Sunderland at Roker Park.

15/1/66 - Stoke City home drew 2-2 (O'Grady, Storrie) att 34,802,
22/1/66 - Bury FA Cup Round 3 won 6-0 (Lorimer 3, Reaney, Greenhoff, Giles) att 30,384,
29/1/66 - Sunderland away lost 2-0 att 35,942.

Albert was dropped after the defeat at Sunderland and he felt like he was made to feel like the scapegoat. He would go on to miss the following thirteen games and it wouldn't be until April that he returned to the side.

With Leeds sitting third in the table, Albert was recalled to the team for an important fixture against high-flying Chelsea after a damaging 1-0 away defeat at Blackpool. It felt good for Albert to be back in the side, and an impressive 2-0 win did his confidence the world of good and was the beginning of a return to the form he was capable of. He kept his place in the starting line-up for the next game away at Fulham on April 8 when he scored his first league goal of the season in a 3-1 win.

Leeds lost the return home fixture four days later against Fulham 1-0, but Albert was back on form. At home against the old foes of Everton, Leeds produced a dazzling display and Albert was on the scoresheet again in a 4-1 win in front of Leeds lowest home league crowd of the season (25,200, the highest was against Manchester United 49,762). In the next game, Albert made his debut in European football when Leeds were defeated by Real Zaragoza in Spain 1-0 before he scored in the return leg a week later in a 2-1 home win in front of 45,008 fans.

4/4/66 - Chelsea home won 2-0 (Bremner, Hinton og) att 37,784,
8/4/66 - Fulham away won 3-1 (Bremner, Johanneson, Storrie) att 38,960,
12/4/66 - Fulham home lost 1-0 att 33,968,
16/4/66 - Everton home 4-1 (Charlton, Lorimer, Storrie, Johanneson) att 25,200.

He missed the next five games through injury but came back for the last game of the season in a 1-1 draw with Manchester United at Old Trafford. One of the games Albert missed was an impressive 3-0 away win on 5 May 1966 at Arsenal's Highbury ground when Jim Storrie scored twice and

Jimmy Greenhoff scored the other. The most notable part of the game though was the attendance of only 4554, the worst ever for a competitive men's home game at Arsenal. Although Leeds were second in the league, Liverpool had already clinched the title, and Arsenal were struggling in fourteenth under Billy Wright. Arsenal fans were staying away in protest at the way the club was run, and heavy storms were forecast. To add to the stay away factor, unusually for 1966 a live game was being shown on television; the Liverpool versus Dortmund (1-2) Cup Winners Cup Final at Hampden Park. It was the second lowest top flight attendance Leeds have played in front of in their history. The lowest top flight attendance was in 1929-30 when a meagre 3,950 turned up at Elland Road to see Leeds beat Sheffield Wednesday 3-0 on 19 April 1930.

19/5/66 - Manchester United drew 1-1 (Reaney) att 35,008.

Albert's second season in the first division had been a disappointing one on a personal level, after only playing 12 league games and scoring two goals he felt he was being overlooked by Revie. It appears that this period can be seen as the start of his demise, through his lack of self-belief and a fragile personality it led him down the path to a reliance on alcohol.

But Albert was still a Leeds player and he was determined to try and gain his place back on a more consistent basis in the new season to come.

Leeds had finished runners-up in the league again, this time to Liverpool who won with a comfortable six point gap, (Liverpool 61 points Leeds 55), but they had shown they were serious challengers and not to be taken lightly. After only playing in twelve league games in 1965-66, Albert took the summer to try and sort himself out and get back into the athletic shape he was used to being in. His intention was to gain full fitness and to try and shake off the niggling injuries he had been picking up.

1966 had some good news for Albert with the birth of his second daughter Alicia. Albert idolised his two daughters who he called his princesses, doting on them both, but even the absolute love he had for Norma and his two children was unable to steer him away from his eventual reliance on alcohol.

It is said that belief, next to talent, is a sportsman's triumph, Albert had all the talent but would ultimately lack the belief. Billy Bremner summed up Albert's situation when he said: "It was as if Albert couldn't believe it was happening to him, as if he thought a black man wasn't entitled to be famous."

Photo: Leeds United Squad 1965-66, Albert front row far right.

1966-67 ALBERT'S EUROPEAN RECORD

1966 was a golden year for English football with the national team lifting the World Cup for the first time in its history.

Alf Ramsey, the manager of the victrious England team gave his verdict on Albert's abilities: "There was no comparable footballer of his type in Europe, maybe George Best, he was a one-off."

In the domestic game, Leeds were now being seen as serious contenders in both England and Europe.

The First Division was a strong competitive league in 1966, with eight teams looking at the possible chance of lifting the title: Manchester United, Nottingham Forest, Tottenham Hotspur, Leeds, Liverpool, Everton, Arsenal and Chelsea all fancied their chances of finishing as champions.

Leeds got off to a bad start to the new season with a 3-1 defeat away at Tottenham. Albert didn't play in the Tottenham game but was picked for the first home game against West Bromwich Albion.

Leeds picked up their first points of the season with a 2-1 victory, and they followed that up with an impressive 3-1 home win against a strong Manchester United side which included, George Best, Bobby Charlton and Denis Law in front of the biggest home crowd of the season, 45,092.

Albert played a major role in the game, providing a pinpoint cross from the right wing for Paul Reaney to head a very rare goal to give Leeds a 2-0 half-time lead. George Best pulled a goal back in the second half with a fine right footed shot, but a bullet like strike from outside the area by Peter Lorimer gave Leeds a deserved victory.

Albert picked up a knock in the game and missed the following 2-0 away defeat at West Bromwich Albion. He returned again for the next game in which they drew 1-1 away at Burnley, which started a run of nine games that Albert would play in. They got back to winning ways with a 2-1 home win against Sunderland with Albert scoring his first goal of the season before he was substituted. His goal proved to be the winning goal in front of 37,646 fans.

24/8/66 - West Bromwich Albion home won 2-1 (Bell, Giles) att 35,102,

27/8/66 - Manchester United home won 3-1 (Madeley, Reaney, Lorimer) att 45,092,

3/9/66 - Burnley away drew 1-1 (E. Gray) att 30,757,

7/9/66 - Sunderland home won 2-1 (Giles pen, Johanneson) att 37,646.

Albert played in a 1-1 draw at home to Nottingham Forest and a 1-0 home win in the League Cup second round against Newcastle. A run of four consecutive draws followed, and a 3-0 defeat at Aston Villa left Leeds floundering in thirteenth place in the league table. Albert had seemingly put the nightmare of the cup final behind him but he kept picking up niggling injuries meaning he would miss games, losing any chance of momentum.

He played and scored in the first of the four draws in a game away at Fulham (2-2) and the following two draws; at home to Everton (1-1) and 0-0 away at Stoke. The League cup third round saw Leeds draw away 1-1 at Preston North End, a game in which Albert didn't play. He returned to the starting line-up for the disappointing 3-0 defeat away at Aston Villa and in a 3-0 victory in the League Cup replay at home to Preston North End.

Alberts run in the side continued with a much needed league win against Arsenal at home 3-1.

10/9/66 - Nottingham Forest home drew 1-1 (Gray) att 35,634,
13/9/66 - Newcastle United League Cup 2 won 1-0 (Peacock) att 18,131,
17/9/66 - Fulham away drew 2-2 (Lorimer, Johanneson) att 19,985,
24/9/66 - Everton home drew 1-1 (Giles pen) att 38,486,
1/10/66 - Stoke away drew 0-0 att 28,987,
8/10/66 - Aston Villa away lost 3-0 att 19,188,
12/10/66 - Preston North End League Cup Round 4 Replay won 3-0 (Lorimer 2 - 1 pen, Greenhoff),
15/10/66 - Arsenal home won 3-1 (Bell, Madeley, Giles) att 31,481.

Albert then played in his first European game of the season against DWS Amsterdam in the Inter City Fairs Cup scoring in a solid 3-1 win in Holland. European football had a positive effect on Albert and suited his fast skilful style of play. In the return fixture against DWS the following week he scored Leeds United's first ever hat-trick in Europe when he netted three times in a 5-1 home victory. He scored the first and second goal early in the first half, and just before half-time with Leeds 5-1 up on aggregate, they were given a penalty for a foul on Billy Bremner. The crowd were pleading for Albert to take the penalty to complete his hat-trick, but Johnny Giles as professional as ever ignored the calls and calmly scored from the penalty spot. Albert was rampant though and DWS could not cope with his speed. The crowd got their wish in the second half when Albert completed his hat-trick to set up another tie against Valencia who Leeds had knocked out in the previous season. Eric Stanger reported on Albert's hat-trick in the *Yorkshire Post*: "Johanneson got the first two goals ... with fine artistry. First he crowned a neat move between Hunter and Madeley and went through the Dutch defence like a dancing master. Then he was in the right spot at the right time to take Greenhoff's through pass and score with calculated deliberation. The crowd rose to him and booed when the South African was denied his chance of a hat- trick by not being allowed to take a penalty five minutes before half time ... A fifth goal did come when Johanneson's shot hit Cornwall's leg on the way and the ball was diverted past Schrijvers."

Albert was flying again, but was brought down to earth in the next game when he was injured in the 1-0 home defeat against Southampton. He was substituted with Peter Lorimer coming on in his place. Albert's injury kept him out for the next four games which included a 7-0 thrashing away against West Ham in the fourth round of the League Cup and a 5-0 away drubbing at Liverpool. The defeats came as a reality check for Leeds who were floundering in tenth place in the league. After the 7-0 defeat, Eric Sangster posed the question in the *Yorkshire Evening Post*:

"Was it a seven-goal wonder or does that thrashing at Upton Park mean that after three successful seasons Leeds United are once more about to sink into the mediocrity which all too often has been there lot in the Football League?"

18/10/66 - DWS Amsterdam away Inter City Fairs Cup won 3-1 (Bremner, Johanneson, Greenhoff) att 7,000,

26/10/66 - DWS Amsterdam home Inter City Fairs Cup won 5-1 (Johanneson 3, Giles pen, Madeley) att 27,096,

29/10/66 - Southampton home lost 1-0 att 32-232.

Thankfully for the Leeds fans the two hefty defeats would be just a blip.

After the two unusually heavy defeats, Revie was glad to welcome Albert back into the team. The week following the drubbing by Liverpool Albert starred in a much needed 2-1 win at home against a West Ham side which included World Cup winners, Bobby Moore, Martin Peters and Geoff Hurst. In revenge for the 7-0 thrashing just over two weeks before Albert produced a match winning performance scoring the winning goal in the 2-1 victory. The win would give Leeds a much needed boost and was the start of an eight game unbeaten run. Although he was drinking and smoking more than was good for him at this point, Albert was still able to hold it together and played in the next four fixtures, including scoring the winning goal in a 2-1 victory away against Newcastle on Christmas Eve in front of 29,160 fans. He missed the 5-0 home win in the back-to-back game against Newcastle two days later on Boxing Day but returned for the 0-0 draw with Manchester United on New Year's Eve.

26/11/66 - West Ham home won 2-1 (Giles, Johanneson) att 37,382,
3/12/66 - Sheffield Wednesday away drew 0-0 att 35,264,
10/12/66 - Blackpool home drew 1-1 (Greenhoff) att 28,466,
17/12/66 - Tottenham Hotspur home won 3-2 (Greenhoff 2, E.Gray) 29,853,
24/12/66 - Newcastle United away won 2-1 (O'Grady, Johanneson) att 29,160,
31/12/66 - Manchester United away drew 0-0 att 53,486.

Albert made a good start to 1967, scoring twice in a 3-1 home win against Burnley, and he also played in the 1-0 defeat away at Nottingham

Forest. But Peter Lorimer recalls the first time he was aware of Albert having a problem with drink saying:

"When things went wrong for Albert it seemed to happen quickly. We played Notts Forest one day, it was a very cold day and he wasn't playing well and he came off at half-time. When we got in the dressing room after we always had a bottle of scotch in the dressing room as me and Bobby Collins used to like a sip before we went out to get the boys going, so there was always a bottle of whisky there, and when we came in, Les Cocker looked and the bottle was almost empty and Albert was sitting in the corner and he'd had a real go at the bottle. I think that is the first time we became aware that he had started to drink."

Four days later he was left out of the mid-week game against Valencia in the first leg of the Inter City Fairs Cup. But he did return to the starting line-up the following Saturday scoring in a 3-1 win over Fulham at Elland Road, and a week later he scored again in a 3-0 home win in the FA Cup third round against Crystal Palace. Although he was on a good scoring run, he was left out of the next two games, a 2-0 defeat away at Everton and the midweek return leg against Valencia which Leeds won 2-0.

Johnny Giles said of Albert's situation:

"He was an amazing player but he kept to himself a lot. In those days, it was all about playing football. The club had no psychologist and offered no help to players who struggled off the pitch. I think if times had been different, Albert's career would have also been different and his life would have taken a different turn."

7/1/67 - Burnley home won 3-1 (Greenhoff, Johanneson 2) att 37,465,
14/1/67 - Nottingham Forest away lost 1-0 att 43,899,
21/1/67 - Fulham home won 3-1 (Giles, Greenhoff, Johanneson) att 32,015,
28/1/67 - Crystal Palace FA Cup 3 home won 3-0 (O'Grady, Bell, Johanneson) att 37,768.

At this point Albert was feeling more and more a fringe player. He made a scoring return to the side in a 3-0 home win against Stoke but missed the next four games. Again the club were saying that he was injured but Albert would claim later that he was fit most of the time. He returned to the side on March 15 in an FA Cup replay against Sunderland but was substituted at half-time due to injury with Terry Cooper taking his place. The replay at Elland Road is remembered due to thousands of spectators being locked out when the turnstiles were shut twenty-three minutes before kick-off. Some fans, desperate to see the action, scrambled on the Scratching Shed roof. Leeds had been unable to make the match all ticket due to the time factor between games. The match kicked off and was only ten minutes old when a ten foot crush barrier at the corner of Lowfields Road and the Scratching Shed collapsed. Many of the fans were startled and some suffered from crush injuries. There was an overflow of fans that spilled beyond the perimeter track and onto the pitch for safety. Referee Ray Tinkler halted the match and a fleet of ambulances took eighteen people to Leeds General Infirmary. Leeds Chairman, Harry Reynolds, appealed for calm on the public address system, and after fifteen minutes, the Police and Tinkler agreed that the match could continue with hundreds of people squatting near the touchlines. The official attendance was recorded as 57,892 which became Leeds United's record home attendance and still stands today.

11/2/67 - Stoke City home won 3-0 (Bell, Lorimer, Belfitt) att 37,370,
15/3/67 - Sunderland home FA Cup 4 replay home drew 1-1 aet (Giles) att 57,892.

Albert didn't play in the fifth round second replay against Sunderland which Leeds won 2-1, and he would only play in one further match in the 1966-67 season. His twenty-second and final league game of the season was a 1-0 home win against West Ham, which meant that Leeds had avenged the earlier 7-0 thrashing to Hammers in the League Cup by beating them twice in the league. Albert was injured in the game and was replaced by Mick Bates. He would play no further part in a season in which Leeds finished fourth in the league and were knocked out of the FA Cup in the semi-final by Chelsea. Injuries and his reliance on alcohol were starting to take their toll on Albert and he was substituted in three of his last four games of 1966-67.

22/4/67 West Ham away won 1-0 (Lorimer) att 25,500.

Albert said of 1967 that he suffered serious damage to his knee ligaments and that the injury never did heal properly. With his speed being a big factor of his game, the injury aligned with his drinking would restrict his appearances in his final three seasons at Leeds. He had appeared in twenty-two league fixtures but his appearances were dwindling as the seasons were passing. Leeds had reached the semi-final of the Inter-City Fairs cup in 1965-66 and had gone one better this season reaching the final. But having lost in the first leg 2-0 away to Croation side Dynamo Zagreb, they were unable to turn the tie around in the second leg which ended 0-0. It left Leeds without silverware again at the end of a long season, after going so close again… but that would soon change.

Photo: Leeds United squad 1966-67

Back Row: Norman Hunter, Alan Peacock, Jack Charlton, Paul Madeley, Eddie Gray, Rod Belfitt.

Middle Row: Don Revie (Manager), Willie Bell, Mike O'Grady, David Harvey, Gary Sprake, Albert Johanesson, Rod Johnson, Jimmy Greenhoff.

Front Row: Paul Reaney, Bobby Collins, Johnny Giles, Billy Bremner, Jim Storrie, Peter Lorimer, Terry Cooper.

1967-68 – UPS AND DOWNS

Going into the 1967-68 season football had become a massive spectacle. With the advent of televised football and the success of Match of the Day (initially first aired in August 1964) football had become big business and more professional. Leeds had been accused of cynical tactics under Don Revie and there were accusations that he was known for encouraging his players to feign injury in order to make a substitution so that he could influence the way that a game was going (between 1965 and 1967 substitutes could only be used as a replacement for an injured player). It is suggested that one of the reasons the Football Association amended the rules ahead of the 1967-1968 season to allow substitutions to be made for tactical reasons, was in response to this form of 'professionalism'.

There were high hopes that the 1967-68 season would be the one in which Leeds would break their silverware hoodoo. On a personal level Albert was still drinking more than was good for him. He said: "Every so often I would pull myself back from the brink and deliver a great performance in training, causing the management to consider giving me an opportunity in the first team." But his appearances were becoming fewer and fewer. Peter Lorimer said of Albert around this time: "A couple of times he did come into training and you could tell he had been drinking, it had got hold of him before he left Leeds."

Albert started the first game of the season in a 1-1 draw at home to Sunderland on 19 August 1967 in front of 36,252 fans.

19/8/67 – Sunderland home drew 1-1 (Greenhoff) att 36,252.

The promising start he had after being selected for the first game was short-lived as it wouldn't be until 7 October before he appeared for the first-team again.

He returned to the side following a mid-week European game in which Leeds had put nine goals without reply against Spora Luxembourg. Leeds continued their goal scoring spree with a remarkable 7-0 defeat against Chelsea at home in which Albert scored in front of a crowd of 40,460.

Phil Brown in the *Yorkshire Evening Post* reported on Albert's goal: "Johanneson sent his fans almost delirious by nimbly notching the first with his head (an event in itself for Albert) in five minutes." *The Yorkshire Post* also reported on the game stating: "Speedy winger Albert Johanneson, recalled to the side, opened the scoring, the rest of the goals came in the order of; Jimmy Greenhoff, Jack Charlton, Peter Lorimer, Eddie Gray, Hinton (own goal) and Billy Bremner." The match would enter the record books as the only match in the history of the Football League to have seven different goal scorers from one team. Marvin Hinton was the unlucky Chelsea player scoring his second own goal in two consecutive seasons at Elland Road.

Albert retained his place for the following League Cup game at Elland Road in which he scored again in a 3-0 win in front of a crowd of 20,927. Leeds ten game unbeaten run came to an end with a 2-0 away win at West Bromwich Albion in which Albert had a rare appearance on the substitutes bench, coming on to replace Jimmy Greenhoff.

He was restored to the starting line-up for the mid-week Inter City Fairs Cup second leg against Spora Luxembourg which Leeds ran out comfortable 7-0 winners for a 16-0 aggregate victory. After scoring another hat-trick Albert is still in the record books as the only ever Leeds United player to score two hat-tricks in any European competition. Six other Leeds players have scored a hat-trick in European competition; Rod Belfitt, Peter Lorimer, Arthur Graham, Tony Yeboah and Alan Smith but only Albert has registered two.

He continued his fine form and goal scoring exploits by scoring in the next match, a 2-0 home victory against Newcastle United which moved Leeds up to fifth in the table. A disappointing 1-0 away defeat was followed by two wins against Arsenal and Manchester United that took Leeds up to fourth in the table. Albert played in the 1-0 away defeat at Sheffield United on 11 November, and came on as a substitute at half-time for Terry Hibbitt in the Inter-City Fairs Cup 1-1 draw at home against Partizan Belgrade on 6 December 1967. The game would mark Albert's last appearance for Leeds in a European game and also marked the beginning of the end of Albert's Leeds career as Don Revie moved Eddie Gray onto Albert's left wing, a position he would make his own.

7/10/67 Chelsea home won 7-0 (Johanneson, Greenhoff, Charlton, Lorimer, Gray, Hinton og, Bremner), att 40,460,

11/10/67 – Bury home League Cup round 3 won 3-0 (Charlton, Johanneson, Greenhoff) att 20,927,

14/10/67 – West Bromwich Albion away lost 2-0 att 21,300,

17/10/67 - Spora Luxembourg Inter-City Fairs Cup Round 1 won 7-0 (Johanneson 3, Greenhoff 2, Cooper, Lorimer) att 15,196,

25/10/67 – Newcastle United home won 2-0 (Lorimer, Johanneson) att 30,347,

28/10/67 – Manchester City away lost 1-0 att 39,713,

4/11/67 – Arsenal home won 3-1 (Lorimer pen, Jones, Gray),

8/11/67 – Manchester United home won 1-0 (Greenhoff) att 43,999,

11/11/67 – Sheffield United away lost 1-0 att 24,715.

Photo: Leeds beat Chelsea 7-0 in front of a bumper 40,460 crowd.

Leeds would end their long quest for silverware when they won the Football League Cup on 2 March 1968 beating Arsenal 1-0 in front of 97,887 fans at Wembley. Terry Cooper scored the winning goal with Eddie Gray playing outside left. Albert by now was out of the picture and not in contention for a place in the side. He would only make one further appearance in the 1967-68 season, when he played in a 3-0 defeat in the last league game of the season when Don Revie put out a reserve side as they could only finish fourth in the league but were still in the Fairs Cup.

11/5/68 – Burnley away lost 3-0 att 13,247.

Leeds still had a semi-final second leg in the Fairs Cup against Dundee to play four days after the Burnley game and the tie was in the balance after a 1-1 draw in Dundee. Leeds would go on and win the semi-final second leg 1-0 at home with the new regular outside left Eddie Gray getting the goal. Leeds went on to play Hungarian side Ferencvaros in a two-legged final. A slender 1-0 win at home with a goal from Mick Jones on 7 August was followed up by a 0-0 draw in Hungary on 11 September to give Leeds their first European title.

Albert only played in nine first team league games in 1967-68 (one as sub), scoring twice, and only in one league cup game in which he scored.

By his own admission he had now had sunk into the abyss, he was drinking regularly in some of the more 'inhospitable and environmentally unfriendly hostelries' where people didn't go to gossip, just drink.

With his football career in decline he found alcohol as an escape from everyday pressures and although he knew he was letting people down, he was unable to escape its clutches.

Les Cocker arranged for Albert's brother, Trevor, to have a trial at Elland Road, but he wasn't offered a contract and Albert felt he had no-one to turn to within the game.

He was still only twenty-eight and having spent seven years at Elland Road, Leeds were the only club he wanted to play for. Some of the other players were advising him to try and find another club, but he didn't want to entertain a move, he said he loved Leeds and even though he had his struggles, felt he was settled there.

Albert said his relationship with Don Revie had disintegrated to the point that Revie rarely spoke to him. He didn't believe that Revie was being racist, rather that he was a man just focused on success. Upon his breakdown in relations with Revie, Albert said: “In the 1960s he (Revie) was just one of an entire population who had no idea of the pressures placed upon a black man in a white society, let alone on the football field. Revie was a selfish man; he simply did what he felt was right for Leeds United and not for anyone else.”

Photo: Leeds United 1967-68

Back Row: Norman Hunter, Mick Jones, Paul Madeley, David Harvey, Gary Sprake, Jack Charlton, Rod Belfitt, Eddie Gray, Mike O'Grady.

Front Row: Paul Reaney, Terry Cooper, Jimmy Greenhoff, Johnny Giles, Billy Bremner, Mick Bates, Terry Hibbitt, Peter Lorimer, Albert Johanneson.

PAUL 'SPEEDY' REANEY

Paul Reaney was a superb full back who played for Leeds for fifteen years throughout their glory years. He was nicknamed 'Speedy Reaney' due to his incredible speed and overlapping qualities.

He was born in London before moving to Yorkshire as a child. Described as 'mixed race' the talented right-back was the first non-white footballer to represent the men's senior England team when he made his debut, coming on as an 80th minute substitute for Keith Newton, on 11 December 1968. The friendly international was played at Wembley and ended in a 1-1 draw, with Geoff Hurst scoring the England goal.

Reaney would play a massive part in Leeds United's history, starring for Leeds throughout their glory years from 1962 to 1977 playing in a total of 734 games. He was an exceptionally quick defender known for his man-marking and overlapping abilities. George Best said of Reaney that he was one of the toughest defenders he ever faced as he "Was quick and liked to get stuck in." While at Leeds Reaney helped them rise as Division Two Champions, and later they would win the Division One title, Fairs Cup, FA Cup and League Cup. After making his historic debut for England in 1968,

Reaney was injured on 2 April 1970 playing for Leeds when he broke his leg away at West Ham in a 2-2 draw. It was a cruel blow, with only six games of the season left to play in a season in which Leeds were still in the hunt for three trophies which included the FA Cup final against Chelsea on 11 April which they drew 0-0, a European Cup semi-final defeat (2-1) to Celtic at Hampden Park on 15 April 1970 and FA Cup final replay defeat (2-1 aet) against Chelsea on 29 April. In the space of only 18 days Leeds ended up finishing the season empty handed. They finished runners-up to Everton who took the title with 66 points to Leeds' 57.

A scant consolation for Leeds was that they did finish top scorers with 84 league goals compared to Everton's 72.

Don Revie said about Reaney's injury: "When Paul Reaney tragically broke his leg in the League game against West Ham at Upton Park, I could have wept… for the boy himself, who had seen his dreams of European Cup, FA Cup and the World Cup crash around him. I could have also wept for Leeds United, he was such a pivotal player."

The broken leg that Reaney sustained, would keep him out for six months and meant he would miss out on a place in the England squad for the 1970 summer World Cup in Mexico.

He eventually made a full recovery and returned to the Leeds side, and although he was regularly selected for England squads (only one sub was allowed in those days) he only received two more caps for England. The last one playing at right-back in a 1-0 away win in Malta on 3 February 1971 in a European Qualifier.

Although playing 734 games for Leeds and being known for his overlapping runs he wasn't known for his goalscoring ability, having scored only nine times in his career - which equates to one goal every 81 games. One quirk of his goal scoring feats though was that Leeds never lost when he scored!

After a spell at Bradford City, he finished his playing career in Australia. After his playing career finished, he ran coaching sessions and made guest appearances at holiday resorts. Reaney had played for 18 seasons at Elland Road in Leeds United's most successful era, and he is still third in their all-time appearance list behind only Jack Charlton and Billy Bremner. As well as being hailed as a true Leeds United legend, Reaney can also be celebrated as a trailblazer being the first non-white footballer to represent the men's senior England national football team.

Photo: Paul Reaney – Back row (fourth from right) in the 1968-69 League Championship winning squad

1968-69 - LEEDS FIRST EVER TOP FLIGHT TITLE

It was clear by now that Albert didn't figure in Don Revie's plans and he had little chance of being selected for the first team. He only made one league substitute appearance in 1968-69 in the third game of the season against Stoke City, coming on for Eddie Gray and scoring what would be his last first team goal for Leeds United.
This was the season that Leeds would go on to be first division champions for the first time in their history.

His only other two appearances of the season was when he started in a League Cup game in a full strength side on 25 September 1968, scoring in a 2-1 over Bristol City at Elland Road in front of 16,359 fans, and an FA Cup replay against Sheffield Wednesday when he scored in a 3-1 defeat.

17/8/68 - Stoke City home won 2-0 (Jones, Johanneson) att 30,383,
25/9/68 - Bristol City home League Cup Round 3 won 2-1 (Johanneson, Jones) att 16,359,
8/1/69 - Sheffield Wednesday FA Cup third Round Replay home lost 3-1 (Johanneson) att 48,234.

Albert managed three goals in three appearances in the 1968-69 season, but he was totally out of favour.

The lack of appearances just fed Albert's insecurities and his drinking continued unabated, still only twenty-nine his fitness was suffering and although the ability was still there, the lightning speed was diminishing.

He had received criticism throughout his career that he somehow lacked courage, but legendary Leeds defender Norman 'bites your legs' Hunter came to Albert's defence: "He was braver than many people gave him credit for, and had the scars on his legs to prove it. On his day he could skin any full-back, but he lacked the consistency and it was unfortunate that Albert was around at the same time as Eddie Gray. He was one of Don Revie's most promising signings but when Eddie got a grip of his place on the wing, something had to give and Albert found himself in the reserves."

He was still receiving support from the likes of Leeds coach, Les Cocker who had been with Albert from the start of his Leeds career and said of him: "The lad had everything, he was blessed with pace, skill and balance, what a player." Cocker advised Albert to knuckle down and show the boss that he was worth his place on the left wing, but Albert said the situation between him and Revie had become almost intolerable and there was no communication between the two.

With Leeds winning trophies and losing their title of 'Bridesmaids', they were in their best period in their history while looking forward to their first ever appearance in the European Cup. Their progression and further ambition was shown when they broke the British transfer fee record when they signed Allan Clarke from Leicester City for £165,000 in June 1969. Albert on the other hand was in freefall, out of favour at Elland Road, his drinking and smoking were completely taking over his life and with the arrival of Clarke, Albert was put on the transfer list. Leeds were asking for a small fee for him which second division Bury were happy to meet, but after speaking with the management at Bury, Albert said it was the wrong move for him. He also had talks with Brighton and Walsall but these talks came to nothing. Albert was in limbo and said of his situation: "Gradually, I lost control of who I was, other people were making decisions for me, unscrupulous people abused my good name and I was associating with the wrong kind of person, I was stumbling from one crisis to another. I felt alone and without any source of comfort other than that found in alcohol."

At this point Albert was still the only high profile black player in the top division a position he had held since Leeds promotion in 1964. A sign of the times was shown with the arrival of the Football League sticker album. The 1967-68 album featured 22 teams with 330 profiles of players of which only one was black. It wasn't until the emergence of Clyde Best who signed for West Ham in 1968 that another black player would regularly grace the first division.

Photo: Leeds squad 1968-69

CLYDE 'BUNNY' BEST

Heavy built and black, Clyde Best did not look like the typical footballer that fans expected to see playing back in the sixties and seventies. On appearance, many would have expected him to be in the boxing ring as opposed to the football pitch.

Clyde's father Joseph migrated to Bermuda from Barbados as part of the merchant navy, and married Clyde's mama Dorothy, a Bermudian from Somerset. Born in Bermuda on 24th February 1951, Clyde gained his first cap at the age of 15 playing for the Bermudian national team. At 18, Clyde was signed for West Ham United and played his first match against Arsenal on 25th August 1969. He went on to play 188 League games for West Ham, scoring 47 goals between 1969 and 1976. It was an exciting time for football, but a difficult time to be a black player. Best had to play amidst a lot of racism and hooliganism.

He was beloved at Upton Park where he said he felt generally safe, but he said that away games were fraught with tension.

Clyde got his nickname from a local sports broadcaster Joe Brown, who, when announcing a game called him 'Bunny Best' (Clyde's sister's nickname) but the name stuck, and he continued to use it thereafter.

Upon his arrival at West Ham in the 1960s, he was looked after by legendary club captain Bobby Moore. He credited Moore and fellow West Ham players Harry Redknapp and Billy Bonds with helping him deal with racist abuse he received.

He said of the abuse: "There'd be monkey chants and booing every time I touched the ball. But I always found the best way to silence everyone was to put the ball in the net."

The title of Best's autobiography, The Acid Test, comes from a letter he received containing a threat that someone would throw acid in his face as he came onto the field. He says his own mental toughness and team support helped him to deal with the threats he was receiving. "I wasn't only playing for myself, but for every person of colour in England. I knew that if I could put in a good performance, I was doing my job. When I look now and see all the players of colour that are playing in England, hey, that makes me happy." Clyde distinctly remembers the fear when he opened the acid hate mail letter. It was the 1970-71 season and the letter said that when he ran out on the pitch the next day, acid would be thrown in his face. He knew why. That season had been particularly bad for racist abuse. Leeds and Everton were clubs that stood out in Clyde's memory for the roar of monkey chants that would greet him. He was only nineteen at the time and he said: "When you're a young player and you're giving the best you can — and then to be given a letter like that, it's mind-boggling." Thankfully the threat proved to be nothing more than a cowardly scare, but to a teenage player, the threat in itself was very unsettling.

Clyde would go on to be one of the three black players who for the first time appeared in the same Football League team together. The match saw the visit of Tottenham Hotspur to Upton Park on 1 April 1972. The three players in question were Clyde Best, Ade Coker and Clive Charles. Clyde said in his autobiography: "In terms of career milestones, 1 April 1972 has to go down as a special landmark when Ron Greenwood became the first manager to select not one, not two, but three black players in the same league game: Clive Charles, Ade Coker and myself all lined up in a 2–0 victory at Upton Park. It was April Fools' Day and the cynics no doubt questioned whether we were really playing or had just been sent out to warm up. Ron was a pioneer in every sense of the word and later selected Viv Anderson as the first black player ever to appear for England. For all the recognition of Greenwood as a great coach and motivator, he struck an equally telling blow to those who thought the colour of our skin was an impediment to our ability to play."

Greenwood picked his players on merit, and it was almost six years before West Brom's celebrated black trio, Laurie Cunningham, Brendon Batson and Cyrille Regis (nicknamed the Three Degrees) would play together for West Bromwich Albion.

Clyde said of the game against Tottenham: "We didn't really look at it as three black players in an otherwise white team. It was more a case of, hey, we're all mates together. I think most English clubs back then were naive and scared to give black players a chance. Some of the best players in the world – like Pelé and Eusebio – were black but in England we didn't get the same opportunities as we do now."

On racism in general he said: "It's a shame in life when a person looks at the colour of your skin and doesn't like you. It's unfortunate that we have people like that in the world, but that's life. I was brought up to remember that in order for you to like me, I have to treat you the same way I want to be treated myself."

Clyde had a very successful career at West Ham playing in 221 matches and scoring 58 goals from 1968 to 1976. One appearance included deputising for an injured Bobby Ferguson in goal against Leeds United in April 1973 in a 1-1 draw.

The regular racist abuse that Clyde suffered took its toll on him "psychologically," and he suggests it is part of the reason why he left West Ham to play for Portland Timbers in the United States at the relatively young age of 25. Having taken English football by storm for eight years he left England for North America where he played for Cleveland Force, Toronto Blizzard and Los Angeles Lazers. He played in a combination of indoor and outdoor football during the eight years he spent in the US footballing world, playing against some of the greatest-ever footballers, including Pele, Johan Cruyff and George Best.

Clyde said of his career: "So I'm happy with what I've done and I know that I paved the way for a lot of players of colour and I'm just glad I had an opportunity to do it and that people could learn from it. The game belongs to everybody and everybody has a right to play.

In 2004, Clyde received a Fifa Order of Merit Award, and was awarded an MBE in 2006. He also had a stint managing the Bermuda national team between 1997 and 1999.

Photo: Clyde Best towards the end of his West ham career in 1975. Back Row fourth from the right

1969-70 ALBERT'S LAST SEASON AT LEEDS

Albert's last season at Leeds United was the 1969-70 season which started well when they won their first ever Charity Shield trophy, beating Manchester City 2-1 at Wembley. In another strong season, they would finish runners-up to Everton in the League, and reach the FA Cup Final where they were unlucky to lose 2-1 to Chelsea in the first FA Cup final replay since 1912.

They also reached the semi-finals in their first attempt at the European Cup, losing an epic tie to Celtic. After losing 1-0 at Elland Road a crowd of 136,505 saw them defeated 2-1 at Hampden Park.

But in such a hectic season in which they were challenging on all fronts, Albert would only play a cameo role, featuring in only two games. In his ninth and final season at Elland Road, he played in a 4-1 defeat away at Derby in front of a crowd of 41,011, in which Revie played a near reserve team as they faced Celtic in the European Cup first leg only two days later.

Albert's second appearance and his very last game for Leeds United became a famous game, not so much for it being Albert's last game for Leeds but for two outstanding goals by Eddie Gray. Don Revie once famously said of Eddie Gray: "When he plays on snow, he doesn't leave any footprints" and in the Burnley game Gray showed why.

In the week leading up to the Burnley match, Leeds had played 5 times. During that week they had lost the League to Everton. They had also been beaten 1-0 by Celtic in the first leg, hampering their chances of making the European Cup final. And with Paul Reaney breaking his leg against West Ham they had lost one of their star players to serious injury.

There was a certain irony in the Burnley game as Albert was selected to play in the number nine shirt, whereas apart from when he was substitute, Albert had previously always worn the number eleven shirt in every game in which he had started for Leeds.

The crowd at Elland Road for what would be Albert's last game was 24,691, and it was held just a week before Leeds were to face Chelsea at Wembley in the FA Cup final. The line-up for Albert's last game was mainly made up of the reserve team:

1. David Harvey
2. Terry Yorath
3. Paul Peterson
4. Paul Madeley
5. John Faulkner
6. Eddie Gray
7. Peter Lorimer
8. Mick Bates
9. Albert Johanneson
10. Chris Galvin
11. Terry Hibbitt
12. Jimmy Lumsden

Only three players would stay in the side for the following week's cup final: Paul Madeley, Peter Lorimer and Eddie Gray.

Eddie Gray scored his two memorable goals, one in the first-half when he lobbed the Burnley keeper from 35-yards. And one in the second half which was a spectacular solo goal, when he picked the ball up outside the Burnley penalty area facing the Scratching Shed (South Stand), and with Albert laid prone in the penalty area, he proceeded to beat four Burnley defenders (two of them twice) before rattling a right footed shot low into the corner of the net.

Albert said of his last game: "I admit I wasn't in the best of ways, having been drinking until the early hours of the day of the game. It didn't help that Burnley kicked lumps out of me and were on my case from the kick off. No matter what I did, I seemed to end up being hacked to the floor or knocked off the ball. In the end I could take no more, I gave up, my knees gave way in the penalty area and I collapsed to the floor. I felt as though I was going to be sick through the effects of the alcohol."

The last vision Albert had as a Leeds player was lying on his back in the penalty area, watching the player who had taken his place craft out one of the greatest goals ever scored. In the video of the goal, Albert can be seen laid prostrate after a tackle in the Burnley area while Gray 'waltzes' around the hapless defenders.

Albert continued: "As I lay on the floor, desperate to be taken off, I watched in awe as Eddie Gray, displayed the kind of skill I once possessed; he weaved past six or seven Burnley players in the penalty area before scoring a great goal. It was an incredible goal, my heart sank as I realised that it could have been me receiving the celebrations at scoring such a wonder goal, instead, I was laid upon the floor feeling sorry for myself."

After he was eventually taken off, he said Don Revie just turned his back and refused to acknowledge him.

30/3/70 – Derby County away lost 4-1 (Kennedy) att 41,011,
4/4/70 – Burnley home won 2-1 (Gray 2) att 24,691.

With Revie refusing to speak to Albert he thought the only way he could communicate with him was by letter. He proceeded to pen a letter to Revie with a full apology for his behaviour and pleaded for another chance, but he said he received no reply from Revie.

After being placed on the transfer list, he asked for a clear the air meeting with Revie and was granted fifteen minutes in his office.

Albert said he felt desperate and was begging Revie not to release him, but he said Revie didn't want to know: "Get out of my office Albert, why are you doing this? You are a bloody disgrace, now get up off your knees and leave me in peace. You are finished here, your time is up, I told you never to let me down but you have too many times now. You're washed up, look at you. There is little or no chance of you getting into my team now, I've got plans and you don't figure in them." Albert left Revie's office distraught.

Throughout his nine-year Leeds United career Albert had played 199 times (171 league, 28 cups) and scored 65 goals (48 league, 17 cups). He had physically played in front of crowds of over four-and-a-half million (4,575,252) and many more millions through television. This was in a time when he would invariably be the only black player playing, and more often than not be only black person in the stadium.

Although it wasn't recognised at the time, Albert blazed a trail for non-white players to make their mark in the game. Playing in front of large crowds and with the advent of television, millions were able to see his achievements. He paved the way to show that it was possible for everyone with the ability, regardless of their background or colour, to be able to make it in the highest level of football. Albert was distraught at having to leave, but he was resigned to the fact that his time at Leeds had finally come to an end. After nine eventful years at a club he loved, he was transferred to fourth division York City for a reported fee of £4,000 in the summer of 1970.

Photo: Leeds United squad 1969-70 with the League Championship trophy

Standing: Don Revie (Manager), Bob English (Physio), Allan Clarke, Mike O'Grady, Jack Charlton, Gary Sprake, David Harvey, Mick Jones, Paul Madeley, Albert Johanneson, Cyril Partridge (Reserves Trainer), Syd Owen (Chief Coach).

Seated: Les Cocker (Trainer), David Walls, Paul Reaney, Nigel Davey, Terry Cooper, Terry Hibbitt, Johnny Giles, Billy Bremner, Mick Bates, Jimmy Lumsden, Paul Peterson, Derek Edmunds.

Front Row: Colin Smith, Robert Malt, Andrew J. Danskin, Stephen Brown, Sean Grace, Jimmy Mann, Bobby Rutherford, Brian Stuart, Philip Thrussell, Peter Hearnshaw.

ALBERT – YORK CITY

Albert tried to see the move to York as a fresh start and he was determined to try to make the best of it, but as he admitted himself, his life was already in a downward spiral. He had put on weight, lost his pace, lost his touch and lost his fitness.

He said life wasn't great in York, he was playing in front of much smaller crowds, but he still faced racist chants from the stands which he said was more noticeable due to the smaller numbers making it feel more personable. Albert said that although his York colleagues were supportive of him, the standard of football was poor compared to what he was used to. Tom Johnston the York City manager said of signing Albert for York: "I couldn't believe it when I signed him for York City, he was easily the most skilful player of his era."

Albert made his York City debut on 4 August 1970 in a 0-0 draw at home to Notts County. Although struggling he did manage to help York get promoted in the 1970-71 season, playing in the first twenty games but he lost his place in November. He was described in the local newspaper as a "Ground breaking sportsman who played with a smile, but unfortunately, his well-documented drinking was already affecting his playing when he joined York City."

He regained his place in the side as the team won promotion after taking the last promotion spot by finishing fourth in the old fourth division.

In one of the games for York Albert recalls being called a 'fat nigger' by someone in the crowd and at the time he said he was as equally offended at being called fat as he was to the racism.

He only played in the opening game of the following season before being released at the end of the 1971-72 season.

The local paper said of Albert's brief career at York: "Undoubtedly one of the most skilful players to ever play for City, unfortunately by the time he joined City, he was suffering in his personal life."

At 32 years-old Albert's football career was finished in England. Albert said on his release from York: "It was all over. My football career crumbled to nothing, York released me because I wasn't fit enough, my weight was getting worse and my drinking habits were getting me into trouble. I wasn't what you would call a pleasant drunk, I often became outspoken towards management and staff. My life became a blur."

After playing at the highest level of English football, Albert's life had disintegrated, he knew he had a problem and at times would attend clinics to try and overcome his alcoholism, but to no avail as he found himself total absorbed by alcohol.

With his football career finished in England he decided to head home back to South Africa in a bid to try and get himself back on the straight and narrow.

ALBERT - BACK TO SOUTH AFRICA

After leaving York City, Albert returned to South Africa in a desperate bid to try to piece his life together again. He signed for Glenville FC in 1972, spending two months in Cape Town, where he revitalised and inspired the club. Glenville would go unbeaten that season and would win the Federation Professional League (FPL) title (Mainstay League), and finally capture the imagination of Cape Town's football fans who up to that point had only supported Cape Town Spurs.

Glenville player Vince Naude said of Albert's time at Glennville: "In 1971, Glenville finished mid-table. In 1972, we were league champions, unbeaten. This was due to the introduction, as a guest player, of the great Albert Johanneson of Leeds United. He revolutionised the training and introduced a more technical aspect to the sessions."

Fellow Glenville player, Keith Arendse said: "Albert Johanneson changed everything. He took the training for the two months he played for us and he revolutionised things. He brought a different perspective, and had us playing to our strengths. He brought an English mentality to our game, and he had us doing things in a professional way. We were the fittest and the quickest in the league, and nobody could beat us that year, in 1972."

"It was a real honour to play alongside him," said Peter Eagles, who was Glenville's captain at the time.

"Albert was known as being a tremendous footballer, character and fun guy to be around. I remember when we arrived at training one day, it was very cold," said Eagles. "So Albert had a stiff few beforehand. I also remember us playing one day and he'd also had a few drinks, and the referee came to me, as the captain and asked, 'what's he on?'

Arendze recollected: "Albert was always lekker (under the influence of alcohol), but he was an amazing guy. You always knew where you were with him and he was quite a funny guy too. Albert was the life of the party during our bus trips to play games in Durban or Joburg. I remember once we had about 12 bottles of Mainstay (cane) in the bus and Albert asked, 'drink it with water…why?' And he proceeded to do a strip by taking off a piece of clothing every time he had a drink. But he was a great guy, he always made jokes, and he was a great footballer as well."

After leaving his mark on Glenville, Albert returned to England hoping to resurrect his football. Still in his early thirties he was hoping to find a new club and to start again.
But he said on his arrival back in England: "In the time I was away, football had moved on and so had life."

With no club or support from the one thing he knew about, football, he had money and no means of support. He took to casual work, washing up in restaurants, cleaning up at a tailors or any other menial jobs that he could find. He said the people of Leeds hadn't forgotten him and he would still be treated to drinks and food wherever he was in the city.
A number of times Albert underwent treatment for alcoholism, but in the end the addiction proved too big a barrier for him to overcome.

ALBERT - POST FOOTBALL

Tarnished Black Flash is back from hell to Elland Road heaven

Wing and a care

FROM the very top to the bottom, ex-Leeds United and York City ace Albert Johanneson has been there. Sports editor MARTIN JARRED charts Johanneson's comeback...

FORMER Leeds United and York City winger Albert Johanneson is learning to stand on his own two feet again - literally.

There have been times in the last few years when the former darling of the terraces has been flat on his back, laid out by drink.

But Johanneson has clawed his way out of the gutter, regained his self respect and is preparing to enjoy a testimonial year, which starts with a sportsman's dinner at Elland Road tonight, more than 20 years after hanging up his boots.

Testimonial organiser David Robinson, who has done much to rescue Johanneson's life, said: "Albert is back. Albert needed help and asked for it."

In recent years Johanneson had turned to drink, but he spent three and a half months drying out at the Chaucer Clinic in London this summer and is now steadily re-building his life.

South African-born Johanneson's tale is one of rags to riches and back again.

A barefoot footballer from Johannesburg, he was recommended to Leeds by a school teacher after starring with his local club Germiston Collies.

He arrived at Leeds on a three-month trial and in April 1961 became one of Don Revie's first signings, making his debut against Swansea, the same month when two goals by Jack Charlton at Elland Road earned a 2-2 draw.

Blessed with exceptional pace, he was dubbed 'The Black Flash' by United fans and was the club's joint leading scorer when they stormed to the Division Two title in 1964.

The following season he became the first black player to play in an FA Cup final as United lost 2-1 in extra time to Liverpool.

He continued to be a force in the all-conquering Leeds side until injuries and the emergence of young Scottish international wingman Eddie Gray effectively ended his career at Leeds.

After about 200 senior appearances for Leeds he arrived at Bootham Crescent in July 1970, still only aged 30.

But his York City displays were fitful and after just 26 League games in two seasons he was released.

He spent some time back in his native South Africa, playing and coaching, but returned to Leeds where his life became enveloped in an alcoholic haze.

Unemployed, he lived in a dingy flat in the Harehills area of the city with his life on a downward spiral. He was in the wilderness for the best part of 15 years.

But with help from his friends, Johanneson has bounced back.

The Professional Footballers Association helped with a £1,800 grant to help him with his new flat in Roundhay and he has started putting something back into the game by coaching children in Leeds.

Testimonial organizer Robinson said: "I am so pleased for Albert. He is such a nice man. It has been the biggest fight of his life."

WELCOME: Skipper Bobby Sibbald (right) greets Johanneson to City

IN FLIGHT: Johanneson leaves a defender trailing

Johanneson file

Born: March 12, 1940.
Height: 5ft. 7ins.; weight: 10st. 3lb.
Leeds United debut: v Swansea Town (home) 2-2 Division Two April 8, 1961.
League: apps 170 (2), goals 48; FA Cup: apps 14, goals 5; League Cup: apps 5, goals 5; Europe: apps 5 (1) goals 3.
York City debut: v Notts County (home) 0-0 Division Four 4 August 15, 1970.
League: apps 26, goals 3; FA Cup: apps 3, goals 1; League Cup: apps 4, goals 1.

Eddie Gray said of Albert's plight after football: "When I was Leeds manager (1982-85), Albert would sometimes come to visit me at the ground. He would tell me that he wanted to start training again, but could not afford to buy any boots. I would give him all the equipment he needed, but I always knew that he really wanted it so that he could sell it and use the money to buy drink.

He continued:

"It was not difficult to be moved by the story of Albert's decline. One day when Linda (Gray's wife) came to pick me up at the ground, we spotted Albert by the main entrance, we gave him a lift into town. During the journey, Albert talked about all the things that had gone wrong in his life. I'd heard it so many times that I had become emotionally immune to it, but it had a big effect on Linda. By the time Albert left us, tears were rolling down her cheeks like a waterfall."

At various times after he had finished with football, his ex-colleagues at Leeds would try and help him with his problems, Peter Lorimer said:
"We wanted to get him to join the former players association, but it was no good. Albert would just go missing." When an event was held at Elland Road in honour of a wheelchair bound Don Revie who had been diagnosed with motor neurone disease on 11 May 1988 (which would be his last visit to Elland Road), Albert was invited to the charity football match with all of his old teammates but he failed to show up.

Peter Lorimer said in an interview on Sky Sports: "The ex-players have an association to help any players that get into trouble, and we actually had a dinner for Albert at Elland Road and we raised quite a bit of money. We'd arranged for him to go into one of the clinics in London which he went into for a period. We brought him out of the clinic to the dinner and there was a great response, a total sell-out. The plan was to get him back on his feet, give him a little bit of money and hopefully things would be okay, but unfortunately when he came to the dinner that night he started drinking again and by the end of the evening, to everybody there it became quite obvious that he might have gone a step too far."
Too ashamed that he had fallen off the wagon, Albert refused to go back to rehab and carried on drinking.

Albert still hit the headlines after he finished playing when John Sadler ran a sleazy two-page expose on him in *The Sun* Newspaper:

'Sunsport Special on the Tragic Story Behind the Forgotten Hero of Revie's Superteam.' With the headline: 'He was Soccer's First Black Prince. Now he's Boozed up and Broke.'

A barefooted Albert was photographed on a bed reading a scrapbook of past glories with a bottle of cider. The unflattering article read 'John Sadler meets down-and-out Wembley ace…'

Looking back on his career and troubles, Albert said of himself:

"Eventually I lost my way and my life spiralled away from me. I'm not blaming anyone else for the problems I had. People said I couldn't handle the pressure of British football, such people have no understanding of what 'real pressure' is, try being called 'gorilla man' by policemen, or being refused entry into a restaurant because you are black and will frighten off white customers. That's the kind of thing I had to deal with virtually every day of my life in England, it gets to you, it impacts on every moment of your waking life. So who could I turn to for help, guidance, support, the manager of Leeds United? I tried him, he laughed at me and told me toughen up or get back to South Africa with 'my own kind.' Genuine pressure isn't playing football or running a pub or being a freeloader because of your status in a city, it's much more serious, it's about constantly living in fear of attack, making life or death decisions, protecting families, caring for people."

Albert's decline into alcoholism cost him the thing he loved the most in his life, his family. Norma had tried to support Albert through his difficulties and drinking, but concerned about what effects Albert's erratic behaviour was having on their two young daughters, she decided to leave him and move back to Jamaica, before moving on to America.

After moving away from England with their mother when Albert's drinking became impossible to live with, it was a lot for the two sisters to cope with. Eventually relocating to the United States, as they got older they tried to reconnect with their father when they had heard that he was struggling and virtually desolate. Alicia said: "There are really no words to describe the depth of sadness and grief we feel about that, especially when, as we grew older, we made several attempts to get in touch with him, only to have all inquiries into his whereabouts turn to dead ends."

Photo: Albert in happier times 1962-63

ALBERT – EPITAPH

Tragically, Albert was unable to conquer the grip that alcohol had on him and he was found dead in his flat in Leeds on 28 September 1995. His cause of death was given as meningitis. It is debatable that while he was still alive, Albert didn't receive the recognition that he deserved and most of headlines focused on his problems with drink rather than the incredible life and football career he had. He was buried on 9 October at Lawnswood Cemetery in Leeds. More than 100 mourners attended the funeral, including his two daughters and a number of former team mates. The Yorkshire Evening Post ran the headline on his death 'Paupers grave for Soccer hero Albert, Sad discovery as VIP tribute is prepared. Initially after not having a headstone for his grave, Albert's youngest daughter Alicia explained the situation: "While my sister, Yvonne, and I were in Leeds attending my father's funeral we arranged with Leeds United to have the headstone that currently marks his grave made and inscribed with the Maya Angelou poem, which we chose to put on it knowing from whence our father came and what he achieved in his short football playing career. The club paid for the headstone to be made, and ensured that it was placed on the grave once completed."

Albert's grave is inscribed with a section from the American poet, dancer, singer, activist and scholar Mary Anjelou's famous poem, *Still I Rise.* Albert's eldest daughter Yvonne said of Albert's life: "Despite the humble beginnings from which he came, he engendered hope in others as a pioneer and brought pride to his race. Today, in spite of the fact that many have tried to disregard his contribution to the sport, his legacy can never die, as the poem says, ‘Still I Rise’.”

Still I Rise – Mary Anjelou:

Out of the huts of history’s shame
I rise
Up from a past that’s rooted in pain
I rise
I am a black ocean, leaping and wild,
Welling and swelling I bear the tide.

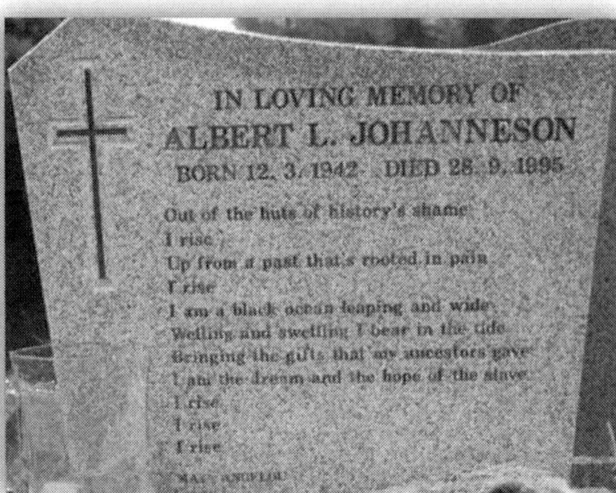

Bringing gifts that my ancestors gave,
I am the dream and the hope of the slave.
I rise
I rise
I rise.

His daughter Yvonne would later say of her father:
"It is not a secret that my dad suffered from alcoholism which affected his marriage. When the situation became too difficult for my mother, we returned with her to Jamaica in 1975. My mother and her sister subsequently moved to the United States in the 1980s and I joined her with my family in the late 1990s." Albert remained in England with little contact with his family. But Yvonne was to see her father again when she was a postgraduate student in France in 1984.

Yvonne continued: "My sister and I would very much like my father to be remembered for the joy he brought to the people watching him play. We firmly believe Albert should be recognised for the contribution he made in football as a pioneer, who like Arthur Wharton, Andrew Watson and Walter Tull, paved the way for the black footballers. Although his influence was most prominent in England, we would also like his legacy to be known in the land of his birth, South Africa. Lucas Radebe and Philemon Masinga are names synonymous with British Premier League football in South Africa, we feel that Albert should be equally recognised by his countrymen as a trailblazer who paved the way."

Twenty years after his death and fifty years after his historic FA Cup final appearance, the Football Association joined forces with the Professional Football Association and Football Unites, Racism Divides project to commemorate Albert's appearance in an FA Cup Final. Albert's daughter Yvonne, and granddaughters Samantha and Stephanie, presented the National Football Museum in Manchester with his runners-up medal in May 2015. The family were flown in specially by the Football Association from Atlanta, Georgia in the USA, and after presenting Albert's medal on Thursday they travelled to Wembley on Friday before attending The FA Cup Final as special guests on Saturday 30 May 2015 to watch Arsenal beat Aston Villa 4-0 from the Royal Box. Yvonne said of the events and summed up Albert's life perfectly: "When you add up all the things my father endured: living as a child in a home with alcoholism, growing up in an apartheid society, transplanted from poverty with little preparation, receiving praise from some fans on the one hand, and overt prejudice from others on the next; falling prey to the same alcoholism, which he tried to fight early on in his career, which then leads to his losing his marriage, his children, his home, his livelihood… it's a lot to deal with."

The extremities of facing admiration and hero-worship one day and horrific abuse and racism the next, would be difficult for any man, but for someone as shy and as reticent as Albert it was enough to push him over the edge. After initially avoiding alcohol he came to rely on it more and more. Yvonne said of his descent into alcohol: "My mother says that as far as she can recall, my father began to drink when his team-mates invited him out after games. At first, she said he had told her that he didn't want to go out, but eventually he did, I guess to build the necessary camaraderie with his team-mates."

While studying in France in the 1980s, Yvonne made a visit to Leeds to catch up with Albert. She said: "I actually spent a night with him at his home. It wasn't the best place, but he fixed up the front room for me and made sure I had clean sheets, a hot meal and an egg and bacon breakfast in the morning. He was very protective and constantly reinforced the importance of my keeping fit and healthy… no smoking and no drinking."

Yvonne and Alicia only found out that there had been a history of alcoholism in the Joahanneson family, when they were visited by a childhood friend after they moved to America. They said: "He told us that our father's father, 'grandad' who used to live with us in Leeds, used to drink heavily and would become quite violent when he did. When he told us we realised how cyclical alcohol addiction and the disturbing patterns it can cause in some people can be hereditary. Our hearts really bled for our dad, especially when relatives told us that he used football as his escape from the turmoil in his home." Unbeknown to Alicia and Yvonne, late in Albert's life he asked Freddy Apfel, a local lawyer and friend, to look after his medals so he wouldn't sell them in times of trouble or should anything happen to him.

Yvonne said: "It meant more than the world to know that he had kept the medals intact and wanted me and Alicia to have them, given that his addiction had kept us estranged for most of our lives. He obviously knew their value and treasured them dearly."

Alicia adds: "For me, more than the medals symbolising his success as a footballer, they reflect his love for us and that's all one could ask for really."

In 2015, fifty years after Albert's historic debut in the FA Cup Final, Albert's family loaned his commemorative medal to the National Football

Museum. Other items of Albert's to go on display included a tankard, which was used in celebration after winning the First Division during the 1968/69 season, an FA Cup Final celebration banquet menu and fan mail sent to Albert by a Swindon Town fan after he impressed during a performance for Leeds against Swindon.

Photo: Albert in action in the 1965 FA Cup Final

Subsequently it was a lot for the two sisters to deal with. After having to leave the family home when the drinking became impossible to live with and ultimately relocating to the US, their trauma was intensified by desperate attempts to locate their father when they found out he was virtually destitute. Alicia says: "There are really no words to describe the depth of sadness and grief we feel about that, especially when, as we grew older, we made several attempts to get in touch with him to help him, only to have all inquiries into his whereabouts turn into dead ends."

Yvonne remembers fondly the family outings to Harrogate and York in Albert's pride and joy – his Rover 2000 – trips to the cinema, long drives into the country and regular visits to restaurants to indulge Albert's love of food from around the world. The contradictory mix of racism and adulation was difficult to handle for a shy man who, when he came to the UK, initially struggled with the notion that black people could officially have equal status with whites. Finding it hard to cope, he leaned more and more on the bottle. Yet Albert didn't drink at all when he first arrived in Leeds. Yvonne says: "My mother says that as far as she can recall, my father began to drink when his teammates invited him out after the games. At first, she said he had told her that he didn't want to go out, but eventually he did, I guess to build the necessary camaraderie with his teammates."

As alcohol began to exercise more influence over Albert's life, his career began to wane. By 1974, Norma could no longer put up with the drinking and the behaviour and moved the family to Jamaica and then the US. Alicia never saw her father again, something which haunts her to this day.

Yvonne did see him once in the 1980s when, while studying in France, she made a visit to Leeds, she said: "I actually spent a night with him at his home, It wasn't the best place, but he fixed up the front room for me and made sure I had clean sheets, a hot meal and an egg and bacon breakfast in the morning. He was very protective and constantly reinforced the importance of my keeping fit and healthy... no smoking and no drinking."

The sisters only belatedly learnt there was a history of alcoholism in the family after a childhood friend of their father's visited them in the US. "He told us that our father's father, 'grandad' who used to live with us in Leeds, used to drink heavily and would become quite violent when he did. When he told us we realised how cyclical alcohol addiction and the disturbing behaviour patterns it can cause in some people can be. Our hearts really bled for our dad, especially when relatives told us that he used football as his escape from the turmoil in his home."

Before their trip to Wembley in 2015, Yvonne made a visit to the National Football Museum in Manchester to deposit some mementoes from her father's career. Unbeknown to Alicia and Yvonne, late in Albert's life he asked Freddy Apfel, a local lawyer and friend, to look after his medals so he wouldn't sell them in times of trouble or should anything happen to him.

Yvonne says: "It meant more than the world to know that he had kept the medals intact and wanted me and Alicia to have them, given that his addiction had kept us estranged for most of our lives. He obviously knew their value and treasured them dearly." Alicia continues: "For me, more than the medals symbolising his success as a footballer, they reflect his love for us and that's all one could ask for really."

ALBERT JOHANNESON – THE FIRST BLACK SUPERSTAR COMIC BOOK

In order to tell the story of Albert's inspirational life, in 2015 Football Unites Racism Divides (FURD) worked with Cape Town illustrator, Archie Birch to publish a 24-page comic book. The comic book was designed to reach a wide and especially young reading audience.

The comic book was the second in the FURD series of comic books following on from the first successful book on Arthur Wharton.

ALBERT HONOURED WITH A BLUE PLAQUE

In January 2019 Leeds United along with the Leeds Civic Trust, honoured Albert with a blue plaque before a Championship match against Derby County. The plaque was officially unveiled by Samantha Jones, granddaughter to Albert Johanneson, along with Brian Deane and Councillors Judith Blake and Jane Dowson.

Photo: Albert's blue plaque is permanently sited outside the East Stand reception at Elland Road

Legendary Leeds born Leeds United player Brian Deane spoke at the ceremony on the impact Albert had left in his wake in English football.

Brian said: "What people don't realise is what he would have had to have gone through to actually get to the point where he was actually in a club situation, it's no mean feat, you know? If you ask me about Albert himself, you know, Albert was probably the generation before the generation that I looked up to, the likes of Cyrille Regis and Laurie Cunningham, and perhaps he was the one who they looked up to. So from that point of view, he's a very important figure in the game for black players, but also for this club (Leeds). You know, to say he was here so long, he must have been some player, with everything that would have been going on in those days, he would have had to have been some player to have the career that he did here."

Leeds United chief executive Angus Kinnear said before the event: "It will be fantastic to have Samantha, Albert's granddaughter, with us on Friday to unveil this special plaque in honour of the first black footballer to play in an FA Cup final. Albert is a massive part of the history of Leeds United Football Club; he was a trailblazer and paved the way for other black players to make their mark on the sport, this is a fantastic occasion for the club as we enter our centenary year."

The plaque reads:

'Albert Louis Johanneson - Born and raised in South Africa, he found a new life in England. A mesmerising left winger, he made 200 appearances for Leeds United from 1961 to 1969 scoring 67 goals, playing an integral role in helping the club win promotion to the First Division in 1964. In 1965, he became the first black African to play in an F.A. Cup Final. 1940-1995.'

The plaque was displayed on the Elland Road pitch before the Championship match against Derby County in January 2019, after which it was sited outside the East Stand reception at Elland Road.

ANDREW WATSON – FIRST BLACK INTERNATIONAL

Photo: Andrew Watson (Top second from left) in the Queens Park team

Andrew was born in Georgetown, Demerara, the capital of British Guyana to a wealthy Scottish sugar plantation owner, Peter Miller Watson, and a local black Guyanese woman called Hannah Rose. Andrew had a fascinating life, he would inherit his father's fortune which was made as a sugar planter, benefitting directly from the slave trade

After arriving in Britain, Andrew was educated in the English public school system. After his father died in 1869, he was left an estate worth in excess of £35,000 (a fortune in those days). The money was shared between Andrew, then aged 13, and his sister Annetta (a small amount was also left to their mother in Guyana). This set up Andrew financially for life giving him the advantage of being able to devote a large amount of his time to football. As well as his business interests, in 1874 he signed for the Glasgow-based Maxwell before moving to the Govan-based Parkgrove FC where he was also match secretary. He acquired a reputation as one of the most stylish, pacey and composed full backs in the Scottish game. Andrew was not only the first person of colour to play football in Britain, but he was also the first to hold an administrative role within a British team.

On the playing side, Andrew became one of the best known and most influential footballers of his day, captaining Scotland and leading his team to monumental victories over England and Wales. On the world stage he is widely recognised as the first black international footballer when he played as an amateur for Scotland three times in the 1880s.

He would also go on to be a player and secretary of one of the biggest clubs in Britain, Queen's Park, a team that achieved two Scottish Cup wins. Queen's Park was one of Scotland's most successful clubs, and also had a reputation as being the club of choice for the social elite.

With Andrew holding the position of secretary, it gives a strong indication of his social status in Scottish society. Eventually he moved south to play for a number of English clubs and forged a respectable and successful amateur career. He saw out the end of his time as an amateur player at Bootle FC between 1887 and 1892. Although residing in England made him ineligible to add to his three caps for Scotland.

Andrew was an early trailblazer, with his feats including being the first black captain of an international team, the first player of colour to win a major footballing competition and the first black player to appear in the English FA Cup. The list of footballing 'firsts' makes Andrew Watson one of the most significant figures, not only in the British game, but in world football.

Andrew's status was acknowledged by the Scottish Football Association when they inducted him into the Scottish Football Hall of Fame in 2012.

EDDIE PARRIS- FIRST BLACK INTERNATIONAL FOR WALES

Eddie Parris (1911-1971) is a name that is often forgotten when recalling the early black footballing pioneers. Eddie was born in January 1911 to mixed race parents, his father John Edward Parris was a telegraph wireman from Barbados and his mother, Annie Clarke was from Leicester. Eddie's father had moved to England in around 1900 when he met Annie who he married in 1909. They moved to Wales and Eddie was born on 31 January 1911. His father served as a signalman with the Royal Engineers in the First World War and was awarded a Victory Medal. He served in Newport in Wales, which was the scene of race rioting directly after the War.

Race riots occurred when discharged soldiers and sailors of colour who had contributed to the efforts of World War One were brought back to Britain to take up permanent residence. This increased the minority ethnic population in Wales, especially in seaport areas like Cardiff, Newport and Barry.

At the end of the war there was a jobs and housing shortage which created racial animosity and led to a series of race riots all over Britain. Tensions erupted first in Glasgow, in January 1919, then boiled over into parts of England, like London, South Shields, Hull, Salford, Liverpool, and eventually Wales. Another factor that exacerbated growing racial tensions between black and white men was the perception that these black men were fraternising with local, white women. This incensed many white men, who actively began targeting and violently attacking black men for having relations with, or marrying white women. Days of rioting ensued and the local police had to call in military support. The government eventually responded with a repatriation drive of people of colour, however not everyone was willing to leave. Many had married and begun raising families in Britain. Wales had become their home, their country.

The Parris family were settled and stayed in Wales where Eddie was making a name for himself in the local footballing world. At aged sixteen he was playing for Chepstow Town in the Gloucester Leagues as a left winger. After some impressive performances Eddie was signed by Bradford Park Avenue making his debut in the second division in 1929, before going on to be Park Avenue's top scorer in 1931-32, scoring 13 goals in 36 appearances which was no mean feat for a left-winger. Park Avenue went on to finish sixth in Division 2 in 1931-32.

After impressing at Bradford in the early part of the 1931-32 season, Eddie who had been born in Pwllmeyric in Wales was selected to represent the national side in an international match against Ireland. With very little publicity or fuss, Eddie became the first black player to represent Wales in an international. The match was played in December 1931 and at twenty years-old it would be Eddie's one and only cap. The 4-0 defeat to a strong Ireland side in Belfast put paid to him appearing in any future internationals. It was thought at the time that Eddie was the first black player to represent one of the Home Nation sides, but it was later discovered that it was Andrew Watson who took that title when he played for Scotland in an international against England on 12 March 1881.

After his Wales appearance, Eddie moved from Bradford to AFC Bournemouth (where he would play in 104 Third Division South matches), Luton Town, Bath City, Northampton Town and Cheltenham Town.

The outbreak of the Second World War halted his career with him only in his late twenties. He finally settled in Gloucestershire working at a local aircraft factory finishing his footballing days playing for the factory team.

Eddie made 268 league appearances in total and scored 60 goals, but he is best remembered as the first black player to represent Wales.

Eddie died in Sedbury in 1971 aged 60.

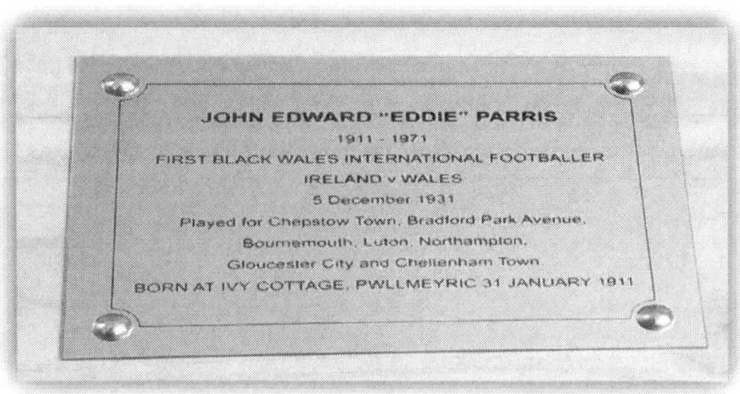

TONY COLLINS - FIRST BLACK FOOTBALL LEAGUE MANAGER

Tony Collins (1926-2021) was born in London, on 19 March 1926 to a 17-year-old unmarried white mother. His father, who was black, was not named on the birth certificate. At the time being an unmarried mum with a mixed race child was seen as shameful and so Tony was adopted and raised by his maternal grandparents.

Tony was a promising schoolboy footballer, but the outbreak of World War Two in 1939 put paid to his early career. He served three years doing wartime service as an Army driver while stationed in Italy. On his return to England he signed for Sheffield Wednesday although he didn't make any first team appearances at Hillsborough.

After moving to York City in July 1949 he went on to make ten appearances for them in the Third Division North. He was transferred from York to Watford in 1950 for a fee of £250 (approx. worth £7,000 in 2023) where he spent three years making ninety appearances and scoring eight goals.

After Watford, Tony joined Norwich City in 1953 (29 appearances and 2 goals) and when the Norwich manager Norman Low decided that all his team should be over six feet tall, Tony lost his place and was transferred to Torquay United in 1955 (89 appearances and 18 goals). He briefly returned to Watford in 1957 where he made a further seventeen appearances scoring one goal, before signing for Crystal Palace later that year; becoming the first black player to appear for Palace. In June 1959, he joined Rochdale, which would be his final club as a player, where he made forty-seven appearances scoring five goals. In total, Tony made 333 Football League appearances, scoring 47 goals, before he retired in 1961.

In his last year as a player he became player/manager of Fourth Division Rochdale in June 1960, making him the first non-white manager of a Football League club. He became a full-time manager when he retired from playing in September 1961.

In only his second season as a manager Rochdale reached the League Cup Final, only to lose 4–0 on aggregate to Second Division Norwich City in what remains Rochdale's only ever cup final appearance. Tony remained as Rochdale manager until 1967 when he resigned saying the demands of the job took too much of his time and was devaluing his family life,
He remained the only Black manager to have worked in league football until Keith Alexander became manager at Lincoln City in 1993.

His achievements were recognised in 2017 when Tony was awarded the League Managers Association (LMA) Service to Football Award at the 25th LMA Annual Awards Dinner.

Despite his achievements as a manager, Tony became more renowned for his scouting work during a career that spanned six decades.

After he left Rochdale, he took the less demanding role of assistant manager and scout for Bristol City, before he moved on to be chief scout at Leeds United for the legendary Don Revie.

When Revie took over as England manager in 1974, he asked Tony to prepare scouting reports on oppositions teams for players to read. One of the scouting reports was on Scotland ahead of a 1974/75 British Home Championship match at Wembley in which England recorded a resounding 5-1 win against the auld enemy, while perfectly executing advice from Tony's scouting report.

He said of the report: "Don gave each player a copy and the match went exactly as I thought it might. But afterwards one of the England players left their report behind. The papers got news of it and came up with the name 'Super Spy'." It led to the title of a biography co-written by his daughter, Sarita Collins, titled *'Tony Collins – Football Master Spy'*.

The book states that as mixed-race footballer in the 1950s, he faced many challenges. His daughter Sarita found 13 job applications her father had sent during his time as Rochdale manager - he didn't receive a single reply.

Collins' talent for player-spotting was sought throughout the game. As well working with Don Revie, he also worked with Jock Stein, Ron Atkinson and briefly, Sir Alex Ferguson.

Upon his death aged 94 in 2021 the League Managers Association (LMA) chairman Howard Wilkinson said of Collins: "Tony was a true pioneer of the sport. He should be remembered and revered for his achievements on and off the pitch."

THE FIRST BLACK TEAM TO TOUR ENGLAND

In September 1899 an association football team from Bloemfontein in the Orange Free State, South Africa, arrived in England for a tour of the United Kingdom. The team comprised 16 black South Africans who played under the auspices of the whites-only Orange Free State Football Association and was the first ever South African football team to tour abroad. The tour involved playing 49 matches over a four month period against opposition in England, France, Ireland, Scotland and Wales.

The first game was played at St James' Park, Newcastle, between Newcastle United and the Orange Free State Kaffir Football Club. The game was watched by 6,000 spectators, with the South Africans losing the game 6-3. This marked the first occasion a South African association football team had played abroad.

A lot of the people would turn up to watch out of curiosity, with the newspapers reporting on the event in racist tones. In April 1899, *The*

Football Echo, in an article titled; *'The Latest Football Sensation'*, asked the question 'what sort of football will these dark beauties play?'

The Cape Times wrote on 21 September 1899: 'It is hoped that the English sporting press and public will take the same view of such a burlesque of the game as the niggers are bound to provide… The governing body of the Association football seems to have quite ignored the proceedings in connection with this nigger troupe. This is all very well in a way, and no doubt silent contempt is often the best way [of] treating matters unworthy of notice, but the present case is, we submit one of which a very great deal of notice should be taken. The question is, what attitude did the Orange Free State Football Association take up in this matter, and how was it that the organizers of the tour were allowed to slip out of the country with their hirelings almost unheeded?'

On arrival in Britain, and even before the first ball had been kicked, racist cartoons were published in the local press with *The Northern Echo* calling the team the 'representatives from "Darkest Africa".

The Cape Argus ran an article:

'The whole affair is farcical as it is unsportsmanlike, and smacks very much of hippodrome. Western Province "socker" enthusiast can scarcely credit the fact that a gang of Kafirs should seriously be expected to give an exhibition worthy of the name, and the British football public will soon realise this fact. Probably the 8 enterprising financiers will rake in the shekels, but every white man south of the Zambesi not directly interested in the venture will regret the whole proceedings.'

In the Newcastle game it became obvious that the South African's would be no match for the highly rated British opposition. The side played with enthusiasm but 'the spectators in fact laughed more than they would do at the most successful comic opera on the boards'.

The Football News called them 'alleged footballers'. The team went on to lose against Sunderland, Middlesbrough and Scarborough (5-3), (7-3) and (9-3) respectively, in front of crowds ranging between 2,000 and 4,000 people.

There was an imbalance to the tour, the touring side were pitted against the premier professional and amateur teams in Britain, against whom they had little chance of success. The South African team won only one of its forty-nine matches on tour, in a game in northern France against the Sporting Club Tourcoing in Roubaix. Watched by a large crowd that included amateur players from Brussels and Paris, the South Africans enjoyed their only victory winning by three goals to one.

After a game played against Hibernian in Scotland, which was watched by 3,000 people, the *Scottish Sport* wrote: 'To treat the game between the Kaffirs and Hibs seriously would be one door off sacrilege, and to endeavour to find excuses for the persons to blame for inducing our clubs to give them fixtures would be an unpardonable breach of public confidence… it would in all humility and seriousness suggest that the Kaffirs and the 'lady footballers' should combine their forces… and stump some less civilised part of the world than Great Britain – France, for instance'.

Although they only recorded the one victory they went down in history as the first South African football side to play abroad and despite the trying circumstances of racism, ridicule and humiliation reported in the British press, the team was fêted and well-supported throughout its tour.

STAN HORNE - THE FIRST BLACK FOOTBALLER TO WIN ENGLISH FOOTBALL LEAGUE MEDAL

Born in 1944, Stan started his football career in the youth team at Swindon in 1960. He moved to Aston Villa in 1961 playing a further two years in the youth league. He was given his full professional Villa debut in 1963 by manager Joe Mercer (who would later take charge of Manchester City and as Caretaker manager of England) just before his 18th birthday.

He was only the second black player to pull on the claret and blue jersey of Aston Villa after William Clarke.

Stan made six first-team appearances at Villa until he was transferred to Manchester City in 1965.

His final season at Villa Park had been spent in limbo, after club doctors told him that he had serious issues with high blood pressure. He was advised to retire early from the game, and after only six appearances for Villa his contract was cancelled.

After leaving Aston Villa, Joe Mercer took on the role of Manchester City manager in 1965 and immediately offered 20-year-old Stan, a month's trial beginning in September. Having been told a year earlier that his health would suffer if he continued to play, Stan was given further tests and was cleared to resume his playing career again by club doctors.

City won promotion from the Second Division by five clear points in 1966, and in 1968, City did the unthinkable - winning the Division One title finishing two points clear of Matt Busby's Manchester United under the combined management of Joe Mercer and Malcolm Allison.

As a utility player, Stan had frequently covered all manner of positions, stepping in when the team were struck by injury, but he suffered a foot injury himself which restricted his appearances. He made a total of five appearances throughout the season meaning he was not eligible for a medal under the rules at the time. However, a rule change by the Football League since then has enabled players who featured in at least five games to receive a medal.

Stan left Manchester City midway through the 1968-69 season, to join Second Division side Fulham for a fee of £20,000.

Stan eventually became the first player of black origin to receive a league winners' medal… 53 years after winning the title.

It wasn't until 2021, that Stan, along with three other players from that season (Bobby Kennedy, Paul Hince and Harry Dowd) received an exact replica medal of those presented to their teammates at the end of the 1967-68 season.

Stan said of the honour: "When the letter came that I was going to receive this medal, I was absolutely overjoyed, over the blue moon as you might say. It was a fantastic time, playing with some of the best players of that era. The families of the four of us are so proud, you cannot describe it. I cannot dream of anything better. Being recognised is brilliant. We were very lucky to be a part of that team. I am just overjoyed to think that people will now, when they speak to us, say 'you have won a First Division medal', and that is something we will treasure for the rest of our lives. Apart from playing for your country, winning a First Division title medal is as good as it gets. I've always taken great pride from being part of the City squad that won the championship. But when you haven't got a medal to show for it then it feels like other people don't have the same opinion of you. City fans still talk about Colin Bell, Francis lee, Mike Summerbee, Neil Young and Mike Doyle – truly great players. I'm not too sure many of them remember I was part of that team as well. But it's nice to know the club haven't forgotten. To hear City are working on behalf of me and the other players who missed out on a medal is great, even after all these years I will absolutely treasure it."

Stan Horne's place in history is now assured, not only in Manchester City folklore but in the English game as whole as being the first Black footballer to win an English top flight league medal.

JUSTIN FASHANU

Justin Fashanu (1961-1998) was a modern day trailblazer as a boxer, footballer and the first player to declare himself publicly as gay.

As a footballer, in August 1981 he became the country's most expensive black player and the first black £1m player when he moved from Norwich City to Nottingham Forest.

Born in London in 1961, Justin had a tough start to life growing up in foster care in Norfolk with his brother John, who would go on to have his own successful football career most notably in the 'Crazy Gang' at Wimbledon from 1986-1994.

Justin started out as a boxer, reaching two national finals for his age group as a teenager. He was fit, tall, strong, and aggressive. As well as boxing he was also making rapid progress in the youth and reserve football teams at Norwich City, playing as a central striker.

After rising through Norwich City's youth ranks, he broke into the first team age 17, going on to score a magnificent goal against Liverpool which was voted Match of the Day's Goal of the Season in 1980 and gained him legendary status.

In total he played 103 matches for Norwich City scoring 40 goals. While impressing at Norwich he was chosen for the English national under-21 team.

After his record-breaking move to Nottingham Forest in 1981, he endured a miserable season with the team, scoring only three goals. It was during that season that Justin became a born-again Christian and struggled the rest of his life to balance his religious beliefs and his sexuality.

At the time no professional footballer had come out as openly gay but Justin's manager at Nottingham Forest Brian Clough wrote in his autobiography about a dressing down he gave Justin in the Forest changing room: "Where do you go if you want a loaf of bread?' I asked him. 'A baker's, I suppose.' 'Where do you go if you want a leg of lamb?' 'A butcher's.' 'So why do you keep going to that bloody poofs' club?"

The dressing down from Clough and his own emotional and psychological turmoil affected Justin deeply and like many black footballers in that era, he was subjected to racist taunts by fans from rival teams. They would make monkey noises and gestures, and throw bananas onto the pitch. But it was anti-gay prejudice that seemed to hurt him the most.

Justin was aware of what earlier black players had to endure in their lives and said of Leeds United's Albert Johanneson: "Every black footballer of a generation knows of Albert, his football skills are legend. As far as I am concerned, he should be recognised as a hero, a man who battled and had to experience blatant racism that is far worse than any other footballer ever has or, in all likelihood ever will. We shouldn't just dismiss what he did and achieved in a few sentences. Every footballer playing in Britain should be reminded of the perils and dangers of racism, how it destroys innocent people, families and lives."

With the problems he was facing, Justin became erratic and unpredictable, both on and off the pitch. After a serious loss of form and several other incidents, Clough banned him from training and had him removed from the Forest training ground by local Police in October 1982 after Justin tried to defy the ban. Justin then joined Forest's neighbours Notts County in Dec 1982 but suffered a serious knee injury. He then signed for Brighton and Hove Albion in the summer of 1985 but his contract was cancelled in 1986 and he was advised to retire.

But Following an operation in Los Angeles, he had a spell playing professionally in America before returning to England.

In 1990, he became aware that a British Sunday newspaper was about to expose his homosexuality. To counteract the exposé Justin sold his story to the British tabloid newspaper *The Sun*. It was published on October 22 under the headline "£1m Soccer Star: I am Gay." His announcement made him the first high profile footballer to come out as gay.

After Justin publicly admitted he was gay he said there was no support network in football, no one to stand shoulder to shoulder with him.

He continued his footballing career playing for Torquay United, followed by Airdrieonians FC and Heart of Midlothian FC in Scotland, where he enjoyed his most successful period in British football since leaving Brighton.

Although often mocked for being gay by opposing players and fans he was mainly supported by most of his teammates and home fans.

In 1998, Justin moved back to America and became a coach of a new franchise, the Maryland Mania. On March 25 of that year he was accused of sexual assault by a 17-year-old male. After being interviewed by the police, he returned to England saying he would be unable to get a fair trial because of his colour and sexuality. A warrant was issued for his arrest in America, and on May 1 Maryland authorities issued a statement noting that they wanted to interview him. The following day he was found dead in a garage in Shoreditch, London, having hanged himself.

His suicide note denied the charges, claiming that the sex was consensual and that he was being blackmailed by his accuser. Part of the note read: "I realised that I had already been presumed guilty. I do not want to give any more embarrassment to my friends and family."

Justin was cremated with a small ceremony at City of London Cemetery and Crematorium.

Eleven years after his death In March 2009, a football team, *The Justin Fashanu All-stars*, played at a special event supported by the Football Association in Brighton.

The team, which was named in Justin's honour, was created by the Justin Campaign, a campaign against homophobia in football designed to promote the inclusion of openly gay players in football.

Justin was the only male professional footballer to come out as gay publicly way back in 1990, and it would be another thirty-two years before another player announced he was gay when Blackpool forward Jake Daniels declared his sexuality in 2022.

EMMA CLARKE - BRITAIN'S FIRST BLACK FEMALE FOOTBALLER

Photo: Emma Clarke

Emma Clarke was born in Liverpool in 1876, she was one of fourteen children born to parents William and Wilhelmina Clarke. She is considered to be the first black female footballer in England. Life was tough for black people in Emma's era, with racism rife black people were considered second-class citizens, but Emma had a steely determination about her.

At the age of fifteen, she began working as a confectioner's apprentice, but her passion for football was ignited on the cobbled streets of her local neighbourhood.

Her official football career dates back to her first appearance for the British Ladies, the first women's association club team which was founded in 1894 by a mysterious character going by the pseudonym Nettie J. Honeyball. Through an interview with British tabloid newspaper *The Daily Sketch* in 1895, Honeyball declared she formed the football club: "With the fixed resolve of proving to the world that women are not the 'ornamental and useless' creatures men have pictured."

On Saturday, 23rd March 1895, Emma lined up for the inaugural exhibition match, representing the 'South' in their game against the 'North'. On the game the *Daily Sketch* wrote: "All through the afternoon, train-loads of excited people journeyed over from all parts, and the respectable array of carriages, cabs, and other vehicles marked a record in the history of football. Yet all that this huge throng of ten thousand had gathered to see was the opening match of the British Ladies' Football Club."

Though Emma's 'South' team lost 7-1 to their northern opponents, the game is recognised as the first fully fledged women's game to be played under football's founding association rules.

Enthusiasm in the late 19th century for the women's game was high, with thousands of supporters attending matches, and although it was often negatively covered, it prompted widespread press coverage.

Football was not seen as suitable for females to play, with the kit they were forced to wear; bonnets, specially tailored high-heeled boots, and corsets hardly suitable for an athletic event. The first record of a women's football match dates back to 1881, an international match between England and Scotland which took place on 9th May 1881 at Easter Road, the home of Hibernian F.C. Eleven days later, another game was played in Glasgow in front of 5,000 people, but was abandoned after hundreds of men invaded the pitch and the players had to flee in horse-drawn carriages.

In 1895, both Emma and her sister Jane joined Graham's XI on a tour of Scotland in 1896, led by Helen Graham Matthews, who was more famously known as Mrs. Graham. Emma and her sisters were said to have earned around a shilling a week each playing football, plus food and lodgings, which was a substantial amount for a working-class family at the time. The tour would often draw larger audiences than their male counterparts, and included playing at Newcastle United's St. James's Park, and even at the old Wembley Stadium.

Little is known of Emma Clarke's life in or away from football after 1903. But her legacy is assured as the first Black woman to display her sporting talent in the public domain. Emma and the rest of the ladies' football team was a trailblazing entity and they were seen as way ahead of their time.

The women's game continued to flourish until the early 1920s when the Football Association invoked a ban on women's football, stating that: "The game of football is quite unsuitable for females and ought not to be encouraged". The ban was still in force until it was lifted in 1971.

In 2019, a blue heritage plaque commemorating Emma was unveiled at Campsbourne School, Hornsey, which is the site of her team, the former Crouch End FC.

VIV ANDERSON

Viv (Vivian) Anderson was born July 1956 in Nottingham. He would go on to be officially declared as the first person of African descent (his parents were from the West Indies) to play for England's national football team. Viv's parents, Audley and Myrtle were both from Jamaica. Audley came to England in 1954, while Myrtle arrived in 1955. Although there was a lot of racial tension in Britain at the time, Viv said his childhood was relatively untroubled by discrimination.

It was England manager Ron Greenwood who selected Viv for a friendly in 1978 against Czechoslovakia which England won 1-0 in front of 92,000 fans. Ron Greenwood said on selecting the first black player: "Yellow, purple or black — if they're good enough, I'll pick them." Viv said of the occasion: "On the day of the game, I remember getting this telegram from the Queen and one from Elton John in the dressing room, so it was obviously a big thing for people, but I just wanted to go and play. I would love to say I knew there and then that I would be visible and important for other black kids, just as Clyde Best had been for me. But at that point, I was mostly just concerned with getting in the team and the game, if I'm honest."

Viv's first two caps were in friendlies with his third appearance being his first competitive international as England defeated Bulgaria 2–0 at Wembley in a qualifier for the 1980 European Championships. During his career, Anderson would go on represent the England's national team on thirty occasions.

Standing at over 6 feet 1 inch tall, Viv was known as "Spider" for his long legs and his ability as a strong tackling defender. He began his professional football career in 1974 with Nottingham Forest as a fullback, and became a fixture in Brian Clough's talented Forest teams that famously won the European Cup in 1979 and 1980. Anderson's humorous anecdote on the racism he faced was while warming up away at a game in Carlisle for Brian Clough's Forest in the mid-seventies. After being pelted by apples, bananas and pears, he ran for the dugout. Viv said that Clough ordered him back out. "He told me I had to show them I wouldn't be intimidated — and to fetch him two pears and a banana."

Following 328 appearances and fifteen goals in ten outstanding years with Forest, Viv went on to play 120 games (9 goals) for Arsenal from 1984–87. Having previously been out of the international team the move to Arsenal helped Viv revitalise his international standing and he won six consecutive caps from 1984 and into 1985, including four qualifiers for the 1986 World Cup in Mexico. He scored the first of his two international goals (the eighth in the 87th minute) in an 8–0 mauling of Turkey in one of the qualifiers on 14 November 1984. Viv won three more caps at the end of 1986 as England looked to qualify for the 1988 European Championships in Germany. In one of the games, a 2-0 win over Yugoslavia on 12 November 1986, he scored his second and final international goal. Viv was selected for England in two World Cup squads but failed to get any game time in either of them. In total he was selected for England in four major tournaments but only played in one of them.

After leaving Arsenal he became Alex Fergusons first signing at Manchester United with a tribunal fixing the fee at £250,000. He made 54 appearances (3 goals) at Manchester United before moving on to Sheffield Wednesday from 1991–93 making 70 appearances and scoring 8 goals for them. After leaving Sheffield Wednesday Viv took the role of player/manager for Barnsley for the 1993–94 season, making 20 appearances and scoring 3 goals. He then moved to Middlesbrough as player/assistant coach from 1994–2001 (2 appearances, no goals).

He was awarded the Member of the British Empire (MBE) in 1999, and in 2004 he was inducted into the National Football Museum Hall of Fame.

As the first Black player to play for England the last word on racism goes to Viv: “I don't want to bang the drum about race every two minutes, I never said I wanted to be always known as the first black footballer for England, even though I am very proud of it. But I will speak out about race if I think I'm relevant to a conversation and that people might listen, because I think there's still work to be done.”

Printed in Poland
by Amazon Fulfillment
Poland Sp. z o.o., Wrocław
27 July 2023

19e1a672-22d9-49b6-abec-51e29e17f952R01